LEVEL H

STRATEGIES FOR SUCCESS
in Writing

June Coultas, Ed.D.
James Swalm, Ed.D.

STECK-VAUGHN
BERRENT
PUBLICATIONS

Strategies for Success in Writing
Level H

ISBN 0-8172-7108-2

Published by ©Steck-Vaughn/Berrent Publications, a division of Steck-Vaughn Publishing Corporation.

2 3 4 5 6 7 8 9   RP   02 01 00 99

Credits

Executive Editor: Karen Bischoff

Project Editor: Amy Losi

Assistant Editor: Eileen Gerard

Design Director: Steven Coleman

Design and Layout: Jan Jarvis & Jennifer Coton, *Michael William Printery*

Illustrations: Jack Kershner, *Lancelot Art Studio*

About the Authors

Dr. June Coultas is renowned in the field of education and curriculum development. She has held many positions, including teacher, college professor, consultant, lecturer, and award-winning grant writer. She has written and coauthored numerous educational books, and is well-known in New Jersey as a past president of the New Jersey Reading Association and as the supervisor of several district and state-wide reading and instructional programs.

Dr. James Swalm has distinguished himself in the field of education as teacher, college professor, and administrator. He has developed instructional materials and state-wide tests, published over thirty professional articles, and coauthored many educational books. He has served as the director of several New Jersey reading and basic skills programs and was a superintendent of schools in the state.

Table of Contents

Preface

Our society cannot work well if people cannot read, write, or do math. Testing is one way that teachers can find out how well you are learning these skills. It is the way we measure both your success as a learner and our success as teachers.

The materials in this book have been carefully prepared to help you learn the skills you will need to do well on tests. You will become aware of your strengths and weaknesses, and you can practice the skills that give you trouble.

This book also provides you with test-taking strategies. These strategies will give you that extra edge you need to do well on tests. Our job is to give you the tools you need to succeed. We wish you well!

CHAPTER *One*

Getting Started

You may think that once you leave school, you will not need to write. This just isn't true. You may not do the same kinds of writing as you are now, but you will be doing some form of writing.

For some students, writing is almost a painful task. It is something they try to avoid doing whenever they can. These students are not alone. Many people lack confidence in their writing ability.

All writers struggle to produce a piece of quality writing. It is a lot of work to consider what to say, how to say it, and how to make it technically correct. Professional writers do not create an article, a story, or a book all by themselves. They have people who evaluate what they have written, offering suggestions and advice. They have editors, too, who help them by proofreading and editing their work. So, if you experience difficulty when you are writing, you are not alone. You are in the company of some of the world's best writers.

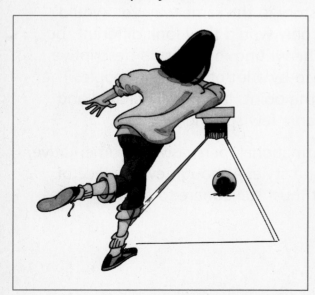

We can compare writing to the sport of bowling. In bowling, you take the ball, focus on the pins, approach the line, and send the ball down the lane. If you are very good, or very lucky, you may knock down all of the pins and score a strike. But more than likely, you will leave some pins standing. You then get another chance to knock down the remaining pins. Unfortunately, even with this second chance, you may leave some pins standing. The game goes on and you repeat the process over and over again.

In writing, you take your pen or pencil, focus on and think about your assignment, approach your task by organizing your ideas, and begin to write. As in bowling, you get a second chance to improve your work. You write your first draft, followed by a chance to rewrite, and then you revise and edit your work.

Although few bowlers ever bowl a perfect game, they keep trying to perfect their skills to achieve that goal. As a writer, you may not produce the perfect paper. However, your work will improve with added practice and revisions.

The Four Types of Writing

It may seem like there are thousands of different kinds of writing. There are science fiction books, social studies textbooks, instructions on how to play a game, newspaper articles on what's happening in Russia, advertisements trying to sell you CDs, writing on cereal boxes, and love letters. Although none of these may seem to have anything in common, all written pieces can be categorized into four types: narrative, informational, persuasive/argumentative, and everyday.

■ The first thing you need to know before writing anything is what you are writing. Often, especially while you are in school, this is decided for you. You are assigned to write a story or a lab report or an essay. However, you also write things that you are not assigned: a letter to a friend, a note to your parent, a list of what you want for your birthday.

■ What you write will determine the form your writing will take. For instance, you would not write a story in the same way you would write a note to your parent. Not only would they look different, but the writing would be different. The writing in a story is descriptive and creative. It is meant to be read by a lot of different people. The writing in a note is short and to the point. It is usually factual and meant to be read by no more than a few specific people.

Each type of writing—narrative, informational, persuasive/argumentative, everyday—has its own general form and style. Although every piece of writing is unique within its category, it must still adhere to the basic rules of that category.

Narrative Text

Narrative text tells a story. Stories can retell actual events, such as biographies, or they can be completely fictional, or imaginary, such as a science fiction novel. They are called narrative texts because they narrate something; they give an account of a real or made-up event.

All narrative texts have the same four basic elements: characters (people, animals, and/or fictional creatures), setting (when and where the story takes place), plot (events that happen), and a theme (the message).

1. List three narrative texts and the reasons they are narratives.

Informational Text

Informational text teaches you something. You read and write a lot of informational text while in school. Textbooks fall in this category. The reports that you write also fall into this category. They are called informational texts because they provide information on specific topics.

As all informational texts contain many facts, before attempting this type of writing you must do research.

2. List three informational texts and explain why they are informational.

Persuasive/Argumentative Text

Persuasive/argumentative text is written to try to bring about change. The writer uses argument, reason, facts, and opinion to try to persuade the reader to do something or to think a certain way. Think of persuasive/ argumentative text as making a case to a jury. Naturally, you would try as hard as you could to make them believe your side of the case. The more persuasive your case, the better your chance that the jury will agree with your position.

Persuasive/argumentative texts use three basic techniques: They appeal to the reader's logic by giving facts and reason; they appeal to the reader's emotions by using descriptive, often colorful, language to inspire feeling; and they try to impress the reader with testimony and/or endorsements from experts.

3. List three persuasive/argumentative texts and explain why they belong in this category.

Everyday Text

Everyday text is useful. The purpose of everyday text is to give you concise information that you need to do or understand something. Some examples of this useful type of writing are as follows: a road sign, a list of rules, a form, a television guide, a menu, or a recipe. These are called everyday texts because they are things that you read everyday.

Everyday texts always have a message to get across. They are straightforward and to the point, and contain very little extra detail, if any.

4. List three everyday texts and the reasons why they belong in this category.

Forms of Writing

Writing can take many forms. It can be a simple note dashed off to yourself; it can be a letter to a company; it can be a report for school; or it can be a novel. Each form of writing has its own style. Letters, in particular, have a special style that you should always follow.

Friendly Letter

When you write to your family or close friends, you are writing a friendly letter. Even though the subject will vary from letter to letter, the form should remain the same. On some writing tests, you may be asked questions about the parts of a letter, how it is punctuated, or which words are capitalized.

Friendly Letter

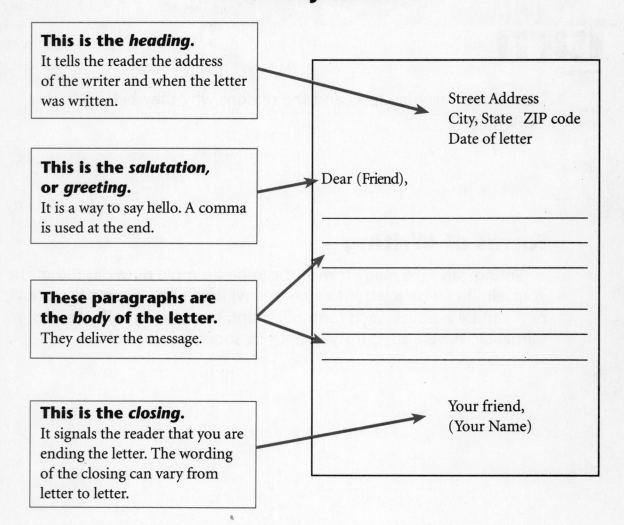

This is the *heading*.
It tells the reader the address of the writer and when the letter was written.

This is the *salutation*, or *greeting*.
It is a way to say hello. A comma is used at the end.

These paragraphs are the *body* of the letter.
They deliver the message.

This is the *closing*.
It signals the reader that you are ending the letter. The wording of the closing can vary from letter to letter.

Street Address
City, State   ZIP code
Date of letter

Dear (Friend),

Your friend,
(Your Name)

ADDRESS ABBREVIATIONS

You should know the standard address abbreviations. Here are some examples of common address abbreviations:

Street Name	Abbreviation	Street Name	Abbreviation
Avenue	Ave.	Boulevard	Blvd.
Court	Ct.	Drive	Dr.
Lane	Ln.	Place	Pl.
Road	Rd.	Street	St.

When you abbreviate the names of states and territories in the United States, there are two forms you can use. The standard abbreviation contains two or more letters and is followed by a period. The post office has its own way to abbreviate state and territory names. Postal abbreviations have only two letters. Both letters are capitalized and there is no period. Below is a chart showing the standard and postal abbreviations for the United States.

State/Territory	Standard	Postal	State/Territory	Standard	Postal	State/Territory	Standard	Postal
Alabama	Ala.	AL	Louisiana	La.	LA	Oregon	Ore.	OR
Alaska		AK	Maine	Me.	ME	Pennsylvania	Penn.	PA
Arizona	Ariz.	AZ	Maryland	Md.	MD	Puerto Rico	P.R.	PR
Arkansas	Ark.	AR	Massachusetts	Mass.	MA	Rhode Island	R.I.	RI
California	Cal.	CA	Michigan	Mich.	MI	American Samoa		AS
Colorado	Colo.	CO	Minnesota	Minn.	MN	South Carolina	S.C.	SC
Connecticut	Conn.	CT	Mississippi	Miss.	MS	South Dakota	S. Dak.	SD
Delaware	Del.	DE	Missouri	Mo.	MO	Washington, D.C.	D.C.	DC
Florida	Fla.	FL	Montana	Mont.	MT	Tennessee	Tenn.	TN
Georgia	Ga.	GA	Nebraska	Nebr.	NE	Texas	Tex.	TX
Guam		GU	Nevada	Nev.	NV	Utah		UT
Hawaii		HI	New Hampshire	N.H.	NH	Vermont	Vt.	VT
Idaho	Ida.	ID	New Jersey	N.J.	NJ	Virginia	Va.	VA
Illinois	Ill.	IL	New Mexico	N.M.	NM	Virgin Islands	V.I.	VI
Indiana	Ind.	IN	New York	N.Y.	NY	Washington	Wash.	WA
Iowa	Ia.	IA	North Carolina	N.C.	NC	West Virginia	W.Va.	WV
Kansas	Kans.	KS	North Dakota	N.Dak.	ND	Wisconsin	Wis.	WI
Kentucky	Ky.	KY	Ohio		OH	Wyoming	Wyo.	WY
			Oklahoma	Okla.	OK			

Note: There are no standard abbreviations for Alaska, Guam, Hawaii, Ohio, and Utah. There are no abbreviations for Samoa.

Standard abbreviations can be used in the address in the heading of a friendly letter. Postal abbreviations are used on envelopes.

Let us look at how we address the envelope for a friendly letter. On the upper left-hand side of the envelope, you should put your name and address. At about the center of the envelope, put the name and address of the person who will receive the letter. Here is a sample:

Ms. Yvonne Dupres
617 Fulton Avenue
Talmoon, MN   56637

Mr. Jacques Montagne
4201 Willow Drive
Lake Placid, NY 12946

5. Write a short letter to a friend, address an envelope, and mail your letter.

Business Letter

If you have not yet done so, you will surely need to write a business letter at some time. Some uses for these letters are to request information, to discuss or complain about a product or service, and to apply for a job. Business letters are more formal than friendly letters, and they are different in form.

A business letter includes a heading, a salutation, the body, and a closing. Unlike a friendly letter, a business letter also includes an inside address. The inside address gives the name and address of the person receiving the letter. Here is an example of an inside address:

Mr. Wilson Tuttle, Sales Manager
Western Sporting Goods Company
5609 North Canal Street
Chicago, IL 66780

Business Letter

Street Address
City, State   ZIP code
Date of letter

Name of Person, Title
Company Name
Street Address
City, State   ZIP code

Dear (Mr./Ms. _____):

_____
_____
_____

_____
_____
_____

Sincerely,
(Your Signature)
(Your Name, Title)

This is the *heading*. It tells the reader the address of the writer and when the letter was written.

This is the *inside address*. It includes the name and title of the person to whom you are writing, the name of the company for which he or she works, and the address.

This is the business *salutation*. A colon is needed after the person's name. If you do not know the name of the person who will receive the letter, the salutation can read, "To Whom It May Concern."

These paragraphs are the *body* of the letter. They deliver the message.

This is the business *closing*. It can vary from letter to letter. It is more formal than the closing of the friendly letter.

It is usually not appropriate to use abbreviations in business letters. However, there are two exceptions. You should use the abbreviation *Mr.* or *Ms.* before a person's name. You can also use the dollar sign ($) indicating the cost of an item. If you cannot type your letter, be sure that your handwriting is legible and that you print your name underneath your signature.

The envelopes for a business and a friendly letter are similar. Your name and address should appear in the upper left-hand corner of the envelope. The center of the envelope should have the name of the person you are writing to, followed by his or her business title, if there is one. (If you do not have a person's name, you can leave this off.) On the next line, put the company name. This is followed by the company address. Here is a sample business envelope:

Mr. Paul Wilson
90802 Parkside Drive
Morrisville, MO 65710

Ms. Rebecca Young, Manager
Customer Service Department
Wheeler & Wilson Corporation
3617 Commerce Boulevard
Indianapolis, IN 46241

YOUR Turn

6. Write a business letter. You could write to the author of a book, someone at a company whose product you own, the principal of your school, or even the President of the United States. Prepare an envelope and mail the letter, if you want.

ADDRESS ABBREVIATIONS

Canadian provinces also have two abbreviations, one standard and the other postal. They are as follows:

Provinces	Standard	Postal
Alberta	Alta.	AB
British Columbia	B.C.	BC
Manitoba	Man.	MB
New Brunswick	N.B.	NB
Newfoundland	Nfld.	NF
Northwest Territory	N.W.T	NT
Nova Scotia	N.S.	NS
Ontario	Ont.	ON
Prince Edward Island	P.E.I.	PE
Quebec	Que.	PQ
Saskatchewan	Sask.	SK
Yukon	Y.K.	YK

7. Imagine that you are planning a trip to some part of Canada. You want to know what to see, where to stay, what to wear, as well as get a map of the area. Write a letter asking for information so you can plan your trip carefully. You can find out the addresses of tourist offices in the different provinces or territories on your own, or use the following address:

Tourism Canada
Industry, Science & Technology Canada
235 Queen Street
Ottawa, ON KIA OH5

(The postal codes for Canada are different from those for the United States. The Canadian codes contain both letters and numbers. The United States codes are only numbers.)

Memos and Notes

When you don't want to write something as formal as a letter, you can write a note. A note is a brief, casual message that you write to your family and friends. You can write a note to a friend to relate something that has happened to you, or you can write a note to your parents to tell them where you're going. You can even write a note to yourself to remind you to do something. Notes are one of the most common forms of writing.

A short business note is called a memo. These messages are brief and to the point. They usually give information or mention something that needs to be done.

A business memo might look like this:

To: Bart Phillips
From: Allan Coleman
Re: Sales Meeting
Date: May 5, 1998

Arrangements have been made for you to attend the regional sales meeting in New Orleans from May 11 to 13. Jean Smith has made your hotel reservations and booked your flight. She'll have all of the details for you on Tuesday morning. Let's meet for dinner Wednesday evening. We should go over our report before our meeting on Thursday. Call my room when you arrive. If I'm out, leave a message at the front desk, and I'll phone you when I get back.

This memo covers just the basics. A memo contains the necessary information and nothing extra.

Other Forms of Writing

As you know, writing can take many other forms. There are books, plays, advertisements, school reports, brochures, menus, and so on. These other forms do not have a structure that is as stylized as letters. Generally, the writer of these pieces decides what form the writing should take. If your teacher assigns you a piece of writing, he or she may determine the form.

Topics for Writing Assignments

In school, you are asked to do a lot of writing. Usually, you are given some guidelines for your writing. You may not realize it, but your writing assignments fall into four categories. These categories are as follows:

- a general topic, probably related to something you are studying.

- a specific topic, again probably related to class work.

- a list of specific topics to choose from.

- free choice to write about anything you want.

There are good and bad points about each of these categories for you, the writer. If assigned a specific topic that you are not interested in, you may find it hard to write. The greater choice you have in your writing assignment, the more chance you have of writing about something that interests you. On the other hand, the more choice you have, the harder it is to choose a topic. It may seem as though you have so many options that you do not know where to begin.

The best strategy to follow when given a choice in writing topics is to pick something you are familiar with and/or something that you find interesting or fun. The more you enjoy what you are writing, the better your writing will be. If you are confused or bored with a writing topic, your writing will be confusing and boring as well.

8. **General Topic:** You are studying the country China in school. Your teacher has asked you to write a report about something relating to China. Come up with three topics that you could write about.

9. **Specific Topic:** Come up with three specific topics that relate to something you have studied this year.

10. **List of Topics:** Pretend you are a science teacher. Come up with a list of three topics that you want your class to chose from for a paper.

11. **Free Choice:** You have to write a two-page essay about anything you want. What are three things that you would write about?

Audience

Once you know what you are writing, the next step is to decide who will read what you have written. The people who will read it are your *audience.* If you are writing in a journal, your audience will be yourself. If you are writing a report for your teacher, he or she will be your audience. Your audience can also be more than one person. Your teacher could ask you to write a story that will be read aloud to the class. Or, you could write an article for your school newspaper that could be read by everyone in the school.

Your audience will have an effect on what you write. For instance, when writing a specific homework assignment for a teacher, you assume the teacher will be the only one to read your writing. You are writing to him or her. You know that your teacher understands the topic you are writing about, so you don't explain every detail.

However, if your teacher let you write about whatever you wanted, he or she may not be familiar with the topic. For instance, if you wrote about your favorite band, your teacher might not know anything about them. You are the authority on the topic, and your writing will explain the information to your teacher.

If you had to write an article for a newspaper, you would be writing to many people. You would need to think about what those people want to know.

Or, let's say your cat had kittens. You want to find homes for the kittens, so you decide to put up signs around the neighborhood. These signs are for a very large audience — your whole neighborhood. Think about what you want to tell them. You want to announce you have kittens for adoption, and you need to explain what to do if anyone wants the kittens. You will also have to think about what you could write that would make your neighbors *want* to adopt a kitten.

Audience Concept Map

The Audience Concept Map can help you visualize the different types of audiences. It can also help you understand how your writing is influenced by the audience who will read it.

Family and Friends: The people you know the best fill the center audience. This includes your family and very close friends. What you write to them is usually in a chatty and less formal style.

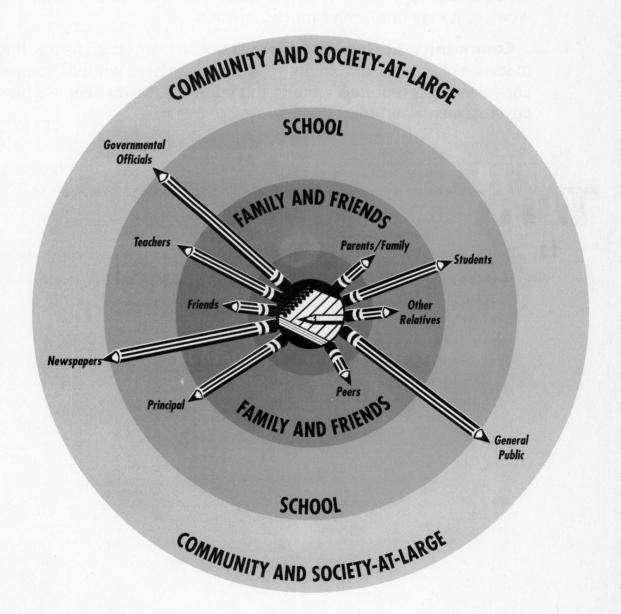

School Audience: This includes all of the people you write for when you are in school. Most of the writing you do for this audience is to fulfill class assignments. Your writing is more formal than when you write to friends or family. You need to pay attention to content, structure, and technical accuracy when writing for this audience.

Included in the school audience are people who may not know you well, such as the principal. When you write to them, it can be to express your views on something of interest to you. You need to give careful consideration to your writing. If it is not well constructed and correctly worded, it may not receive much attention.

Community/Society-at-Large: This is the largest audience. It is made up of anyone who might read what you have written. Book authors and newspaper reporters write to this audience. So do people who write advertisements and road signs.

12. Name three things you have written to each of the following audiences:
    A. family and friends
    B. school
    C. community/society-at-large

CHAPTER *Two*

Getting Organized

In gardening, a common phrase is "plan before you plant." Similarly, you have to plan before you write. That is why prewriting is such an important part of good writing. You must decide on the form your writing will take. You need to know your purpose for writing and the audience who will read what you have written. All of this has to be planned before you put the first words on paper. After that, you can concentrate on what you want to say.

Once you have decided on purpose, audience, and form, you need to organize your thoughts and ideas about your topic. You want your writing to flow smoothly and logically. That way, your audience will better understand what you have to say. There is no one best way to organize information. Some organizational techniques, however, are better for some types of writing than others. You should learn several organizational strategies. This way you can pick the best one for each situation.

Organizing Narrative Writing

When writing a story, you must remember to include these four basic elements: characters (people, animals, and/or fictional creatures), setting (when and where the story takes place), plot (events that happen), and a theme (the message). When organizing your writing, you should outline what you would like these four elements to be. Remember, an outline is only a guideline to help you write. You do not need to stick to it, particularly when writing a narrative text. The story may take on a life of its own, with better ideas being generated than those originally planned.

The most important part of any story is the plot. This is the series of events that make up the core of a story. When outlining a story, it may be easier to start with the plot. Once you have the plot, the other elements— characters, setting, and theme—usually fall into place. There are two models you can use to outline a plot: a story model and a plot line.

Story Model

This outlining technique will help you organize your story in the following way:

1. After the beginning of the story, a problem occurs.

2. Then there is a series of events that lead to a solution.

3. After the problem is solved, there is an ending.

When outlining the model it should look something like this:

Story Model

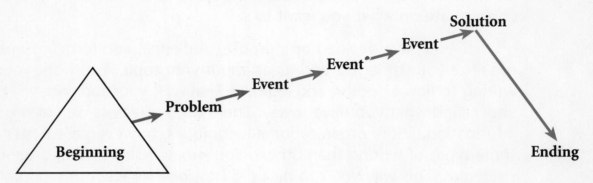

This is just a form for you to follow. Of course, your story may have more or less events. It may also have more than one problem to be solved.

YOUR Turn

1. Come up with an idea for a story. Create a story model of your plot, following the outline given above. Remember, this is just an outline. You do not need to fill in all the details, just the major events. (A story suggestion: Your parents have gone away for the weekend. You and your older brother/ sister are home alone. Something bad happens.)

Plot Line

A *plot line* is very similar to a story model, except the terms are slightly different. In this strategy, you begin with the *exposition*. The exposition is the story's background. It is needed to help the reader understand the plot.

Next is the *rising action* of the story, which are various events. These events lead to a *climax*, which is the most important point in the story. This is when the conflict is brought to a head.

Following the climax, the story winds down. Events occur that help to explain or clarify some points of the story. This is referred to as the *falling action*. Finally, the story ends with the *resolution* of the problem.

Plot Line

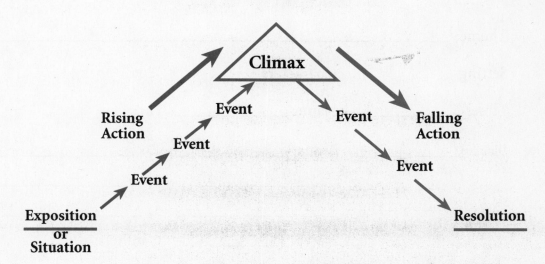

This graphic is meant to give you an idea of what you need to include in your plot. You can include as many or few events as you would like.

YOUR Turn

2. Create a plot line for a story using the outline above. Do not be concerned about using complete sentences. Just tell what happens. You can use the story idea you used in Your Turn 1, or come up with an idea of your own. (Another story suggestion: You and some friends are on your way to a concert. The car you are riding in breaks down.)

Story Map

A *story map* is a great way to outline the key parts of a narrative story. This map will help you highlight all the parts of your story, not just the plot. You can create a story map after you have already outlined the plot, or you can start off with this graphic. It is important to use organizers you are comfortable with.

The story map given here is not intended to indicate how many characters, facts, or events should be in a story. It is merely a way of showing the major points to be considered when you plan your story.

Story Map

Theme: _____

Setting	Characters	Plot
Time: _____	Name: _____	Facts:
Place: _____	Traits: _____	1. _____
	_____	2. _____
	_____	3. _____
	Name: _____	Conflicts:
	Traits: _____	1. _____
	_____	2. _____
	_____	Events:
	Name: _____	1. _____
	Traits: _____	2. _____
	_____	3. _____
	_____	Climax:
	Name: _____	1. _____
	Traits: _____	2. _____
	_____	Resolution:
	_____	1. _____

3. Use a story map to outline a story. You can use the story ideas you used for Your Turn 1 or 2, or you can invent a new story. (A story suggestion: Every day, on the way home from school, a 13-year-old passes an empty, rundown house. One day he/she sees a light coming from the house.)

Organizing Informational, Persuasive/Argumentative, Everyday Writing

The strategies we've given you for mapping narrative writing really can only apply to that form of writing. Narrative texts are the only ones that have characters and a plot. The following strategies can be used for any of the other three forms of writing: informational, persuasive/argumentative, and everyday. These strategies are interchangeable. Some are better for some forms than others, but there are no hard and fast rules. When organizing your writing, use whichever strategy works best for you.

Mapping

Mapping is a way of brainstorming ideas on a topic before writing. You start with a general word or concept in the center of a blank paper. That word or concept is circled. Then you write other words that you associate with that word or concept on the page. Circle them, and connect them to the main word with lines.

The mapping strategy can be used with any form of writing. However, this is a good strategy to use when organizing informational text. This is an especially good strategy to use when writing a social studies or a science report. Shown on the next page is a map that was used to organize ideas for a report on transportation.

Mapping

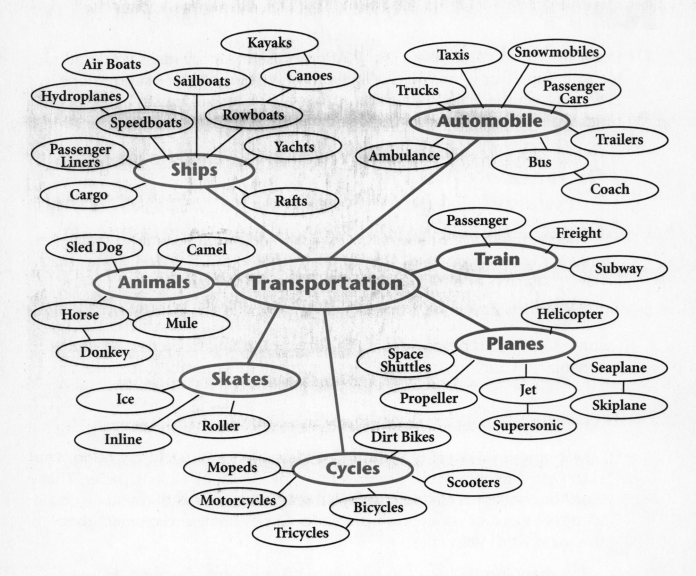

When you start to make a map, no matter what the topic, you will be surprised at how many things you can come up with. As you use this strategy, you will probably find that you know much more about a topic than you thought.

Remember, it isn't practical to include everything from your map in your writing. You can choose to write about the things in only one part of the map. This will make your writing more focused. That is because your attention will be concentrated on a limited amount of information, rather than on too many ideas. The person who wrote the report on transportation chose to concentrate on cycles only.

YOUR
Turn

4. Choose a topic from your science or social studies courses. Brainstorm to create a map showing your thoughts and knowledge on the topic. Do not force the ideas. Just start jotting down things as they come into your mind. Your map will take shape as one idea leads to another.

Chronological Order

Another strategy that's useful when writing informational texts is chronological order. Chronological order means you organize events according to the time or date they occurred, starting with the earliest or oldest event and ending with the last or most recent. You use this strategy when you want to present events in the order in which they happened. Social studies and science reports can be organized in chronological order.

The following is the prewriting organization of a report on the early European explorers of North America.

Early European Explorers Who Visited North America

1000 Leif Ericson was the first European to discover what is now Baffin Island, Labrador, and probably Newfoundland.

1497 John Cabot claimed Cape Breton Island for England.

1534 Jacques Cartier named the St. Lawrence River and claimed Canada for France.

1610 Henry Hudson, after making several earlier trips to North America, faced a mutiny by his crew. Hudson, his son, and seven loyal crew members, were abandoned in what is now Hudson Bay.

1778 Englishman James Cook landed on the Pacific Coast of North America, seeking a water passage to the Atlantic Coast from the west.

1845 British explorer John Franklin set off an extraordinary multi-year search when he and his crew disappeared on his third voyage to find a waterway to Asia. Years later, remains and a diary were found by a rescue mission.

1906 Norwegian explorer Roald Amundsen succeeded in finding a waterway to Asia across the northern reaches of North America.

This strategy is very simple. You briefly list the events you want to write about in the order they happened.

5. Organize some information in chronological order. You can do this with a topic you are writing about for a class assignment. Or, you can pick any topic of your choosing.

Sequential Order

Sequential order is similar to chronological order. It means to organize steps or events according to a sequence, starting with the first step and ending with the last. You use this strategy when something should be written in a certain order. This is especially useful when organizing everyday text. For instance, a recipe or directions for how to make something must be written in a certain order.

Shown is the prewriting organization for directions on how to dye fabric using the batik method.

1. Get materials needed.
2. Put dye into bowls.
3. Melt wax.
4. Paint designs on the cloth with wax.
5. Dip fabric in dye.
6. Dry fabric.
7. Put fabric between layers of paper towels.
8. Iron fabric.

Note how brief the steps are. This is not complete instructions for the batik method; rather, it is just an outline of the basic steps. When writing actual directions, the author will fill in the steps with the details.

6. Organize a task in a sequential order. It can be something you do often, such as making a bed or logging onto the internet. Or, it can be a task you do only once in a while, such as baking a cake or flying a kite.

Cause-and-Effect Organizer

Another helpful way to organize informational reports is by cause and effect. This also works well for organizing persuasive/ argumentative writing. With this strategy, you consider how one thing can lead to another.

Here is an example of a cause-and-effect organizer that you might create for a paper about why smoking is bad for your health.

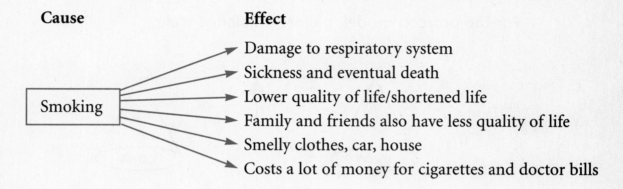

Cause   **Effect**

Damage to respiratory system

Sickness and eventual death

Lower quality of life/shortened life

Smoking

Family and friends also have less quality of life

Smelly clothes, car, house

Costs a lot of money for cigarettes and doctor bills

To create this organizer, you start with a "cause," in this case, smoking. Then you list all the "effects," or things that can happen because of the cause. This organizer is good for persuasive/argumentative writing because it can help you come up with a lot of arguments to support your case.

YOUR
Turn

7.   Use a cause-and-effect organizer to gather your thoughts on any issue. Possible topics are as follows: school uniforms, driving age of 17, coed gym classes.

Pro/Con Model

Another strategy that can aid you in organizing ideas for persuasive/ argumentative text is the pro/con model. This strategy helps you to think carefully about an issue. Before you jump to a conclusion or rush to take a position, you need to weigh the facts carefully. You do not want to write something that you will later regret. This organizer will enable you to see how some facts outweigh others.

For the pro/con model, picture a balance scale.

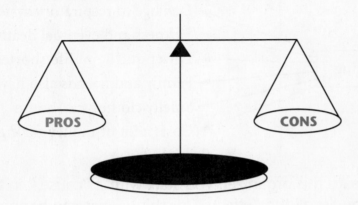

Let's say you had to write a report on recycling. You were asked to take a side, either for or against recycling. Before you write anything, you could use a pro/con chart to organize your ideas.

Pro	Con
less garbage in landfills	store more garbage in homes
reusing materials instead of creating more garbage	takes time to clean & sort recyclables
saves money	there's no immediate gratification for your effort

You place the reasons supporting a position in the "Pro" column and the reasons against the position in the "Con" column. Then you can weigh both sides and decide which side you agree with.

YOUR
Turn

8. Use a pro/con chart to gather your thoughts on any issue. Possible topics are as follows: cutting down the rain forests, banning certain types of music, increasing the speed limit.

Comparison/Contrast Models

Another way to organize your ideas is to use a comparison/contrast model. This is a valuable tool when you are asked to describe how two things are similar (comparison) and/or how two things are different (contrast). These terms are often used together, or the word comparison may be used to indicate how things are similar and how they are different.

On tests or for assignments, it is very important to read the directions carefully. If you are asked to tell how things are similar as well as different, then you must do both to correctly answer the question.

Comparison Model

Let's say, you were asked to tell how frogs are similar to salamanders.

FROGS	SALAMANDERS
amphibians	amphibians
young (larvae) are not like adults	young (larvae) are not like adults
four-toed front feet	four-toed front feet
five-toed hind feet	five-toed hind feet
teeth	teeth
functional eyes	functional eyes
vocal	vocal
meat eaters	meat eaters

Contrast Model

Here are some of the ways that frogs and salamanders are different.

FROGS	SALAMANDERS
Legs used for jumping and swimming	Legs used for walking
Rid themselves of large tails	Keep long tails
Mostly external fertilization	Mostly internal fertilization
Hind legs face away from head	Hind legs face toward head
Teeth usually on upper jaw and roof of mouth	Teeth on both upper and lower jaws and on roof of mouth

Comparison/Contrast Model

In this model, the similarities and differences are shown side by side. This is helpful when you are asked to write about both similarities and differences.

HOW FROGS AND SALAMANDERS ARE ALIKE	HOW FROGS AND SALAMANDERS ARE DIFFERENT
Amphibians	Different skeletal structures
Four legs as adults	Salamanders use their legs to walk; frogs use legs for jumping and swimming
Different species have different colors and sizes	Salamanders have long tails; adult frogs have none
Gills change to lungs as adults	Salamanders have weak voices or are mute; frogs croak loudly
Young do not resemble their adult stage	Salamanders shed their skin; frogs don't

YOUR Turn

9. Pick a topic from social studies or science and construct a comparison/contrast chart on it. If you cannot think of a topic, here are a few suggestions: two ways of doing an experiment; two geological regions; two astronomical bodies; two periods in history; two forms of government; or two important persons.

Venn Diagram

Another way of organizing ideas for comparison and/or contrast is with a Venn Diagram. This is a model with two intersecting circles. The different features of each of the two items are written in the outer portion of the circles. The features they have in common are written in the inner portion, where the circles intersect.

Let's consider the similarities and differences between volcanoes and earthquakes.

VOLCANOES
- Are formed in different ways
- Produce ash and lava
- Can cause mud slides
- Can bury whole cities
- Can cause great weather changes for long periods of time
- Can create islands and new land forms

BOTH
- Occur because of plate movement
- Can cause great destruction
- Occur in the same areas of the Earth

EARTHQUAKES
- Caused by stress on Earth's crust
- Can cause great drops in land surfaces and deep crevasses
- Can cause large structures to sway and topple
- Occur almost every thirty seconds but most go unnoticed by most people because they are mild shocks

YOUR
Turn

10. Use a Venn Diagram to present facts about two things. You can choose any topic.

Outline

Although we have shown you a number of strategies that you can use to organize your writing, sometimes you may not find any of them to be right. In that case, you can come up with your own outline. There really is no one form for an outline. It is just a listing of the main points you want to cover in your writing, as well as the details you will use to back up your main points.

It is helpful to put an outline in sequential order. Think of all writing as having three basic parts: an introduction, a body, and a conclusion.

Introduction states the topic and main idea, of the writing; includes the Who, What, When, Where, How details

Body develops the main idea; this is where you focus on why things are important or why you feel the way you do; the details to support your main idea are included here

Conclusion states the results you want to achieve, how you feel about the issue, what you hope the reader has learned

The following is an outline that a student created for a book report she had to write.

Book Report on *Robin Hood*

1. Introduction
   a. title
   b. history of legend
   c. theme of legend
   d. why I liked it

2. Background of story
   a. an overview of plot and characters

3. Theme of how the poor should be treated fairly
   a. restate theme
   b. explain how theme is portrayed; give at least three specific examples

4. My opinion of book
   a. what I liked and why
   b. what I didn't like and why

5. Conclusion
   a. summary of book
   b. summary of my opinion
   c. to whom I would recommend book

Each numbered item in the outline is a major point the writer wants to cover. The lettered items under each major point are the details the writer could include to explain her major point. This brief outline will give you an idea of one format to use. When creating an outline of your own, include as much information as possible. Remember, you do not have to include all of the outlined ideas in your actual writing.

Your Turn

11. Create an outline for a piece of writing you have to do for an assignment, or create an outline for a book report.

Summary

In this chapter, we have shown you different ways to organize your writing. These strategies will help you get your ideas on paper and organize your thoughts before you begin. Some of these strategies work best with a particular type of writing. Others can be used with several different forms of writing. They are all visual tools to help you get ready to write.

There are three things we wish to emphasize. First, you are not expected to memorize or follow any of these models exactly. They are suggestions on how to organize your ideas or information. Second, your prewriting model will not be a neat product. You will still need to add, change, delete, and reorganize your ideas after you put them down on paper. That is a major part of prewriting. You work out your problems before you start writing. Finally, do not think of prewriting as a waste of time. It is an essential part of writing. It is a way of ensuring that your paper will be logically organized, smooth flowing, and more easily understood by your readers.

CHAPTER *Three*

Get Going

In the previous unit, you read about the importance of prewriting. Now it's time for you to try your hand at writing!

Before writing, think about your topic. Think about what form your writing will take and who your audience will be. You should use a prewriting organizer to help you set up your writing. Once you have your ideas down, you can begin. Remember, you will be writing a first draft. This is your first try. Your writing will not be perfect. There will be changes and corrections that you have to make before you can share your writing with your audience.

Narrative Text

Narrative text tells a story. The types and forms of the stories will vary. Stories can retell actual events, or they can be completely fictional, or imaginary. Here is your chance to write several different types of stories.

YOUR Turn

1. Imagine that you are living during another time. It can be in the past or in the future. Write a story about what your life is like.

2. Write a mystery or a science fiction story. Include yourself among the characters.

3. Write a story about a real event that you or someone you know experienced.

Informational Text

Informational text presents information on a specific topic. An example of an informational text would be a report you write for school. This type of writing may require you to do research on a topic. Sometimes informational writing involves responding to something that you have read or studied.

4. Think about something related to our environment: air pollution, toxic waste, asbestos, oil spills, or anything. Write a report on the problem, including what you think might correct the situation.

5. Write a review of a movie or book that has made an impression on you. In your review, tell what stands out in your mind about the book or movie. You could include why the movie/book would appeal to others.

6. Pick any subject that you are interested in. It can be something that you know a lot about or it can be something that you want to know about. Write a paper on this subject. Include as much information as you can.

Persuasive/Argumentative Text

Persuasive text uses argument, reason, facts, and opinion to try to convince the reader to do something or to think a certain way. The point of persuasive writing is usually to affect some type of change. To do this, the writer expresses his or her point of view and then tries to persuade the reader that this point of view is correct.

While facts and logic are essential ingredients in persuasive letters and editorials, emotions play a part, too. Many people earn their living persuading us to do, buy, or support something. People running for office try to persuade us to vote for them. Advertising firms work for companies trying to persuade us to buy or use their products. We might be persuaded to buy a product if it is endorsed by a celebrity or if we believe it will improve us or make us more important.

7. Pretend you are running for an elected school office. Write a speech that tells your schoolmates what you stand for and why they should vote for you.

8. Many people enjoy riding bicycles. However, because there is a lot of traffic on many roads, riding a bike can be dangerous. Write a letter to a government official suggesting that bicycle paths be created in high-traffic areas so that people can ride safely.

9. Pretend that you bought something you saw advertised. The product does not live up to the claims made in the advertisement. Write a letter of complaint to either the company, the source of the advertisement, or the Better Business Bureau. Also, make a suggestion as to how the situation should be remedied.

Everyday Text

Everyday text refers to things that we read everyday. Its purpose is to give people useful information.

10. Write a set of directions to explain how to make or do something. Remember to list the steps in the order in which they should be done.

11. A girl from another country will be starting school next week. You have been assigned to be this student's partner, to help her get adjusted to your school. Write a list of things that you think would be helpful for her to know.

Unit 3 Revising and Editing Strategies

CHAPTER *Four*

Revising Text

The pieces you wrote in Chapter Three are not finished. They are first drafts. First drafts are not perfect. There is always room for improvement. After you finish writing a first draft, you need to read it over carefully. You must ask yourself how can it be improved and where are the errors that need to be corrected. This is called revising and editing.

- Improving the content of writing is known as revising.

- Correcting technical errors, such as spelling, punctuation, and grammar, is known as editing.

All writers go through these two steps to improve their writing. The better the writing, the more understandable it will be to your audience.

There are many ways to revise a first draft. Sometimes writers do a complete rewrite. However, most times you revise your writing by doing the following:

- adding information

- deleting (removing) information

- rearranging (moving) information

- combining sentences

- adding transitional, or signal, words and phrases

Keep in mind that often there is no right or wrong when revising a draft. Every writer has a style. You will revise your writing according to your personal style. Do not be afraid to practice different ways of revising your work.

Adding Information

When you reread your first draft, you may decide that you left out something that is important. You will most certainly find you need to insert a word or two for clarification or explanation. Do not be afraid to make these changes!

Here is an example of when adding information improves the text:

Draft

> Marc has spoken with the coach about the events he is best suited to run. The coach thinks that Marc will do best running in the long distance races.

The draft leaves a lot of unanswered questions, such as "Why did Marc speak to the coach?" and "Why does the coach think Marc will do best in long distance races?"

> Marc is planning on joining the track team. He
> ~~Marc~~ has spoken with the coach about the events he is best suited to run. The coach thinks that Marc will do best running in the long distance races. He does not have the burst of speed needed to compete in the sprints.

Revision

> Marc is planning on joining the track team. He has spoken with the coach about the events he is best suited to run. The coach thinks that Marc will do best running in the long distance races. He does not have the burst of speed needed to compete in the sprints.

The additions to the draft fill in necessary parts of the story. They complete the picture.

Here is another example:

Draft

> Beth is worried about Tipper. He left early this evening and hasn't come back. She thinks she should call him.

The most important information left out of this draft is that Tipper is a cat. Adding that to the first sentence greatly improves the draft. The writer also decided to add an extra sentence to clear up why Beth thinks she should call Tipper.

Revision

> Beth is worried about her cat Tipper. He left early this evening and hasn't come back. She thinks she should call him. Maybe Tipper will come home if he hears Beth calling his name.

The added information explains who Tipper is and tells the reader more about the situation.

YOUR Turn

1. Revise the draft on the Lewis and Clark expedition by adding information.

> Lewis and Clark needed to obtain information for United States President Jefferson. They would be the first to travel through the territory. It was exciting to see new places.

STRATEGIES to Revise the Draft

Figure out what is missing. Think about what information you need to know to understand what the paragraph is about. Some ideas are as follows: who was part of the expedition, where were they going and why, and what were they trying to find out.

2. Add information to this story:

> People are worried. All the snow from this winter is melting, and it is now raining heavily. The river is getting higher than its banks. Sandbags and levees are needed. Water damage is possible, and people may have to leave their homes.

44

Deleting Information

Sometimes information or sentences need to be deleted from your writing. You might need to keep your writing brief. Or, after reading your draft, you may realize that you don't need to include everything to make your point.

Here is an example of when deleting information improves the text:

Draft

Bryan and Eric are on the same basketball squad. Bryan is two inches shorter than Eric. Eric is good under the basket, while Bryan is excellent on the long shots. Each is trying for the best scoring record. Their coach encourages the rivalry because it gives the team two excellent shooters.

The sentence about the difference in their heights is not connected directly with the rest of this paragraph. Therefore, it can be eliminated. While height can be a factor in this sport, it is not shown to be important in this passage.

Bryan and Eric are on the same basketball squad. ~~Bryan is two inches shorter than Eric.~~ Eric is good under the basket, while Bryan is excellent on the long shots. Each is trying for the best scoring record. Their coach encourages the rivalry because it gives the team two excellent shooters.

Revision

Bryan and Eric are on the same basketball squad. Eric is good under the basket, while Bryan is excellent on the long shots. Each is trying for the best scoring record. Their coach encourages the rivalry because it gives the team two excellent shooters.

Sometimes you need to delete only a few extra words in your writing to make it read more smoothly.

Draft

King Philip stared at the homes of the English settlers in the valley below. This land once belonged to the Wampanoags. King Philip's father, Massasoit, welcomed the English when they came to this land. He thought they would help keep out enemy tribes from his land. Now the English have taken over. Friends have become enemies.

There are too many references to the "land" in this draft. When some of them are taken out, the paragraph will read better. Often a writer needs to include something only once for the readers to understand.

Revision

King Philip stared at the homes of the English settlers in the valley below. This land once belonged to the Wampanoags. King Philip's father, Massasoit, welcomed the English. He thought they would help keep out enemy tribes. Now the English have taken over. Friends have become enemies.

3. Revise the draft below by deleting information.

> The participants were lining up for the parade. It would be the highlight of the week-long festival. Every major organization had a float. Every float had people dressed in beautiful gowns or costumes. These included dancers, singers, and musicians. *Some floats were very small.* It was a wonderfully colorful spectacle.

STRATEGIES *to Revise the Draft*

Which sentence is not in keeping with the rest of the paragraph? Which sentence can be deleted without harming the text?

4. Delete the unnecessary information in the following paragraph:

> The water was extremely cold and choppy. The sailboat was bobbing about, seemingly out of control in the cold and choppy water. Terry thought he could handle the boat in any kind of weather, but it seemed he was wrong. It looked like a typical late summer squall was about to hit before he could make it back to the dock through the choppy water.

Rearranging Information

Sometimes your writing will read better if some sentences or paragraphs are moved to different places in the text. This is known as rearranging, or reordering, information. This revision strategy is especially useful when you are writing something in a sequential or chronological order.

Here is an example of a text that requires some rearranging.

Draft

> When Zack entered the kitchen, it was dark. No one was home. He switched on the light and heard a pop. One of the bulbs burned out. He got a spare bulb from where they were kept. Zack found a flashlight to help him see. It took him only a few seconds to change the bulb. He got the small step-stool from the closet. Soon he was standing in a well-lit kitchen.

The events in this text are out of sequence. The text includes Zack's actions, but not in the correct order.

When Zack entered the kitchen, it was dark. No one was home. He switched on the light and heard a pop. One of the bulbs burned out. He got a spare bulb from where they were kept. Zack found a flashlight to help him see. It took him only a few seconds to change the bulb. He got the small step-stool from the closet. Soon he was standing in a well-lit kitchen.

Revision

Zack entered the kitchen. It was dark. No one was home. He switched on the light. There was a pop. One of the bulbs burned out. Zack found a flashlight to help him see. He got a spare bulb from where they were kept. He got the small step-stool from the closet. It took him only a few minutes to change the bulb. Soon he was standing in a well-lit kitchen.

Sometimes you can make your writing better by rearranging information. Here is a paragraph that will read better after some rearranging.

Draft

Today Rudolph Valentino's name, more than any other, brings forth images of grace, romance, and passion. His sudden death crystallized the fame of this first movie idol. Rudolph Valentino's passionate eyes and magnetic personality were burned forever into his fans' memories.

The first sentence works better if it is moved to the end of the paragraph.

Revision

Rudolph Valentino's sudden death crystallized the fame of this first movie idol. His passionate eyes and magnetic personality were burned forever into his fans' memories. Today his name, more than any other, brings forth images of grace, romance, and passion.

5. Rearrange the sentences in the following paragraph into their logical order.

> Marcy got the best present she could ever hope to receive. The postal delivery truck stopped in front of the Watkins' house. Marcy opened the door when the delivery man rang the bell. She was handed a large envelope. A puzzled expression crossed Marcy's face. She wondered what Nana and Grandpa Watkins could be sending her. The return address indicated it came from her grandparents. She opened the envelope and found a plane ticket and a note from her grandparents saying that they missed her.

STRATEGIES to Revise the Draft

After rearranging the sentences, reread the paragraph to see if it is logical.

6. Rearrange the sentences in the following paragraph to make it read better.

Jack Johnson finished his first day of work on the docks. Johnson suddenly felt nervous. As he gathered his belongings, an eerie darkness settled over the harbor. He knew the waterfront was a dangerous part of town, especially for a 15-year-old boy. He headed up the alley toward the center of town, where he lived. After walking a short distance, he noticed a big, burly man coming toward him. Johnson bent his head and kept walking.

Combining Sentences

There are times when your writing can be improved simply by combining two or more ideas or sentences into a single sentence.

Here is an example of a revision made by combining sentences.

Draft

> Gina wants to buy a new bathing suit. She is in the dressing room trying some on. Her friend Karen is looking at shorts on sale.

There are a number of ways that these sentences can be combined. Here is one possible way of combining them.

> While
>
> ~~Gina wants to buy a new bathing suit.~~ She is in the dressing room trying ~~some~~ on . her friend Karen is looking at shorts on sale.
>
> bathing suits,

Revision

> While Gina is in the dressing room trying on bathing suits, her friend Karen is looking at shorts on sale.

Here is another piece of writing that is improved by combining sentences.

Draft

Kuang loved auto racing. He was saving his money so he could go to the big stock car races. The races were in May.

Like the first example, there are different ways of combining these ideas. Here is one possible choice.

Revision

Kuang loved auto racing. He was saving his money to go to the big stock car races in May.

7. Revise this paragraph by combining sentences.

Canada is the world's second largest country. Only Russia is larger than Canada. Canada stretches from the Arctic Ocean in the north to the United States in the south. In the west, it meets the Pacific Ocean. In the east, it meets the Atlantic Ocean.

STRATEGIES
*to Revise
the Draft*

Look for the short sentences. Those are the ones that can most easily be combined.

8. Combine the following ten sentences into four to six sentences.

> The airport was crowded. It was the beginning of a holiday. It seemed like everyone was traveling. When I checked in at the gate, I learned that the plane was overbooked. The person giving out the boarding passes spoke over the loudspeaker. She asked if any passengers would be willing to give up their seats and take the next flight. The airline would give them a $300 voucher towards the purchase of another ticket. This voucher would be good for one year. It sounded like a good deal to me, and I wasn't in that much of a hurry. So, I volunteered.

Adding Transitional, or Signal, Words and Phrases

Transitional, or signal, words are important in writing. They create a smooth transition from one paragraph or idea to another. They help the reader follow your thoughts. Transitional words give important clues as to the sequence in which things happen. They can also signal a change in the writer's thinking, as well as serve other purposes.

Some transitional words are as follows:

after	first	next
also	however	so
as a result	in addition	suddenly
at last	later	then
because	likewise	therefore
but	meanwhile	when
finally	moreover	yet

You can use transitional words or phrases:

- to combine two sentences

- to help the reader see relationships between paragraphs

- to help the reader anticipate what is coming next

Here is an example of when writing can be revised using a transitional word.

Draft

> Betty wanted to go to the movies. She did not want to go alone.

This sentence would be confusing without the transitional word *but* added to it.

> Betty wanted to go to the movies, ~~She did not want to go~~ alone.
>
> but not

Revision

> Betty wanted to go to the movies, but not alone.

Here is a revision made by adding a transitional phrase between paragraphs.

Draft

> Jason worked at the supermarket bagging groceries. It wasn't a very challenging job, but the hours fit into his school schedule.
>
> Jason was looking for a job that might pay more. Now that he was old enough to drive, he wanted to earn more money so he could buy a car.

A transitional phrase is needed to connect these two paragraphs. The phrase "Despite the convenience of the job," lets the reader know that Jason is not content with his present job and is going to do something about it.

Revision

> Jason worked at the supermarket bagging groceries. It wasn't a very challenging job, but the hours fit into his school schedule.
>
> Despite the convenience of the job, Jason was looking for a new one that might pay more. Now that he was old enough to drive, he wanted to earn more money so he could buy a car.

9. Revise these sentences. Combine them using a transitional word.

> Will felt that he deserved to be on the varsity team. He was not on the team.

STRATEGIES
to Revise the Draft

There is more than one transitional word that could be used here. Choose whichever one you feel sounds the best in the writing.

10. What transitional word or phrase would improve the flow of the text between the paragraphs?

> Tamara and her friends were going to Nelson's surprise birthday party. Unfortunately, the bus was very late. They were concerned that they wouldn't be in time to surprise Nelson.
>
> Val suggested that they forget about taking the bus and call a taxi. She thought that might be the only way they could be sure to get to the party on time.

SUMMARY

You have had the opportunity to learn and practice five important strategies necessary for revising your writing. They are as follows:

- ■ adding information

- ■ deleting information

- ■ rearranging information

- ■ combining sentences

- ■ adding transitional, or signal, words

All of these strategies are part of the writing process. All writers use one, or perhaps all, of them to perfect their drafts. You should do the same.

In the next chapter, we will discuss the editing process. This is another step you need to take in order to polish your writing before it is read by others.

CHAPTER *Five*

Editing Text

Now that we have examined different ways of revising a text, we come to the editing phase of writing. When you edit, you check that you have spelled words correctly, used the correct punctuation, capitalized words where needed, and followed the rules of good grammar and sentence structure. Before you share your writing with readers, you want to check it thoroughly for errors. When you have done this, you are ready to prepare your final draft.

When editing, apply what you already know about the rules of grammar. In this chapter, we will concentrate on three areas of difficulty:

- spelling

- capitalization

- punctuation

When you edit your writing, it is a good idea to check for only one type of error at a time. This will help you be more accurate because you can concentrate on one skill at a time.

Spelling

Let's begin with spelling. No one expects you to know how to spell every word. You should use a dictionary, a spell-check program on your computer, or have someone else read your work.

It is important to check your spelling to avoid mistakes. However, do not let concerns about spelling get in the way of your writing. If you do, you will never expand your vocabulary. If you use the same words in your writing all the time, your reader will lose interest in what you are saying.

There are many ways that you can improve your spelling.

■ Make a list of words that are easy to misspell. Many English textbooks contain such a list. If you study these words, you will learn how to spell them correctly.

■ Write down words that *you* often misspell. You can write these words in a notebook to create your own personal dictionary. Use tabs with letters on them to help categorize the words in alphabetical order. This will make it easier to find words you are not sure how to spell.

■ A similar method is to put words on index cards. The cards can be kept in a card file box, with a set of alphabetical tabs to make the words easier to find.

■ Read your written material backward, from the end to the beginning, and from the bottom to the top of the page. This allows you to look at the spelling of the words themselves, and not the content.

■ Remember that when you use a word-processing program on a computer, the spell check will only tell you if the word is spelled correctly, and not if it is the correct word. For instance, with homonyms like *there* and *their*, a spell check will not be able to tell you when you have used the wrong form of a word.

YOUR Turn

1. Here is a brief passage. Read it and underline all of the spelling errors you find.

> They're are people who beleive in astrologie. They always read the part of the newzpaper that has the horrorscopes. Most people no witch sign they were born under. They look four there sign. Then they reed what is suposed two hapen too them that day. Even peeple who say they don't beleeve in it stil reed there horrorscope.

2. Rewrite the paragraph, correcting all the spelling errors.

Capitalization

After you have corrected the spelling errors in your draft, your next step is to check for errors in capitalization. Let us review the rules for using capitals and show you some of the most common mistakes.

Capitalize the following:

- **Proper nouns** — *a particular person, place, or thing*
  Warren Jones, Jasper National Park, Eiffel Tower

- **Proper adjectives** — *formed from a proper noun*
  Canadian, Californian

- **Historical events** — *names of events, documents, and periods of time* World War II, Magna Carta, Middle Ages

■ **Names of peoples, races, tribes, and languages —**
Rock Dwellers, Caucasian, Pygmy, French

■ **Geographical names —** *planets and heavenly bodies, continents, countries, states, provinces, counties, cities, bodies of water, landforms, public areas, roads and highways, buildings*
North Pole, Mars, Mexico, Atlantic Ocean, Eternal City

■ **Organizations —**
International Red Cross, Boy Scouts

■ **First word in a sentence and a direct quotation —**
Hamlet said, "To be, or not to be."

■ **Particular section of a country —**
Midwest, West Coast

■ **Religions and religious terms —**
Protestant, Islam, Advent, Jehovah, Old Testament

■ **Names and words used as names —**
Grandma Moses, Dad, Aunt Sarah, Dr. Perez

■ **Days of the week, months, holidays —**
Monday, June, Christmas

■ **Official names of businesses, products, and trademarks —**
Rolls Royce, Coca Cola, Kodak

■ **Titles that precede names —**
Prime Minister Denner, Bishop Perkins, General Manager Dillon

■ **First, last, and all important words (nouns, pronouns, verbs, adjectives, adverbs) in titles of books, newspapers, poems, plays, songs, movies, works of art, stories, and essays —**
Moby Dick, The New York Times, "Mona Lisa"

The word *I* is used in place of a person's name and must be capitalized. Words like *mom* and *dad* are capitalized when they are used as names. (I told Mom I would be home at 5:30 P.M.) However, when you use these words as a general reference, they are not capitalized. (My dad is a computer whiz.)

When you are using titles of individuals, capitalize the title only if the person's name follows (Vice President Bailey). If the name is not used, do not capitalize the title (We spoke to the vice president.).

3. This passage has no capitalization in it. Find all the words that need to be capitalized and circle them.

> margaret truman, the only daughter of united states president harry s. truman, writes mystery stories that are set in the georgetown and washington, d.c., area. some of the titles of her books are *murder in the white house, murder on capitol hill, murder in georgetown,* and *murder at the kennedy center.* in reviewing her newest books, the *los angeles times* said, "margaret truman has become a first-rate mystery writer." the *chattanooga times* said, "there are many more locations in washington for murder to happen, and we hope this excellent author will use them in subsequent novels."

Punctuation

Period, Question Mark, Exclamation Point

All sentences end with a *period*, a *question mark*, or an *exclamation point*. A common mistake is using a period after a group of words that do not make a complete sentence. These are called sentence fragments, and they lack a subject (what the sentence is about) or a predicate (the verb).

Comma

The most often used punctuation mark is the *comma*. A comma should be used only to make the meaning of a sentence clearer. It is used to separate words, such as the city and state in an address (Newark, New Jersey) or a series of items in a sentence (Bring your book, ruler, and pencil).

There are three main uses of a comma. You use a comma to separate two independent clauses joined by a coordinating conjunction; to separate who is speaking from a direct quotation; and to separate the introductory word or group of words at the beginning of a sentence from the rest of the sentence.

Let's look at a few examples of these three uses.

To separate two independent clauses joined by a coordinating conjunction

Hillary and Rachel are sisters, and they both attend the same school.

Two independent clauses can be written as two separate sentences. (Hillary and Rachel are sisters. They both attend the same school.) When you join the two ideas to form one sentence, you need a comma after the first clause, before the coordinating conjunction. Common coordinating conjunctions are *and, or*, and *but*.

I told her not to do it, but she wouldn't listen.

■ To separate who is speaking from a direct quotation

> Derrick answered, "I won't be able to meet you until later this afternoon."

The words *Derrick answered* are not part of the quote. They are outside of the quotation marks. These words must be separated from the quote by a comma.

> "I won't go," she insisted.

■ After a word or words introducing a sentence

> Meanwhile, the people were waiting at the station for the train to come.

The subject of the sentence is *the people*, not *meanwhile*. *Meanwhile* is just an introductory word. That should be set off by a comma.

In the following example, a comma is used after an introductory phrase.

> After the fog lifted, the people on board the boat could see the island.

Semicolons and Colons

The *semicolon* is another way to separate ideas in a sentence. When you have two independent clauses and do not use a coordinating conjunction, you need a semicolon. Let's look at an earlier example we used to illustrate the use of the comma.

> Hillary and Rachel are sisters, and they both attend the same school.

If you choose to join these two clauses without the word *and,* you need to use the semicolon.

> Hillary and Rachel are sisters; they both attend the same school.

Another use of the semicolon is to separate groups of words that contain commas within them.

> The class trip was chaperoned by six adults: Mr. Franks, the teacher; Ms. Watkins, the guidance counselor; Mrs. Leland, a parent; Mrs. Abbott, a parent; Ms. Magee, an English teacher; and Mr. Thomas, a social studies teacher.

Without the semicolons, this sentence would be difficult to read due to all the commas. Also notice the *colon* as it is used in the sentence above.

You use a colon before a list or to introduce something that follows, such as in these examples here. However, a colon cannot follow a verb or preposition.

This semester Tonya's courses include the following: French, English I, world history, general biology, algebra, and gym.

Mr. O'Day has traveled to these regions: the French Riviera, the Scandinavian countries, and Great Britain.

Apostrophe

The *apostrophe* is another punctuation mark. While it has several uses, the two most common are to show possession (Mary's book) and to indicate a contraction (don't). A common error people make is confusing plurals that end in the letter *s* (boys), possessives (boy's), and the possessive of a word ending in *s* (boys').

Here are some examples that may help clarify the situation.

> The boys are trying to get the lawn mower started.

The above sentence refers to more than one boy. *Boys* is a plural noun, not a word showing ownership.

> The boy's lawn mower was difficult to start.

This sentence indicates that the lawn mower belonging to one boy is difficult to start. The word *boy* needs an apostrophe before the letter *s* to show possession, or that it is his lawn mower.

> The boys' lawn mowers are difficult to start.

This sentence indicates that we are referring to more than one boy and their lawn mowers are difficult to start. Begin with the plural word *boys*, and then add an apostrophe after the letter *s* to show possession.

Quotation Marks

Quotation marks are another form of punctuation that can cause problems. When a direct quotation ends with a comma or a period, the final set of quotation marks are always placed after the comma or period.

"We should get an early start in the morning," Chuck said.

Jean answered, "I'll set the alarm for five o'clock."

Exclamation points and question marks are placed inside the quotation marks when they punctuate the quotation. But when they punctuate the main sentence, they are placed outside the quotation marks.

Mother asked, "Are you going to be late coming home today?"

Did Dad really mean it when he said, "You're grounded for a whole week"?

Most of the time the final punctuation for a direct quotation will be inside the set of quotation marks. Ask yourself, does the punctuation refer to the sentence itself or to the quote?

4. This passage needs two types of punctuation: periods and question marks. Mark the changes right on the story.

Jason wondered why his friend Todd was not in school He decided to call Todd's home to see why he was absent Jason was surprised when no one answered the phone He decided to try calling again later

After dinner, Jason phoned again There was still no answer Where could Todd be Why wasn't anyone at home Jason was worried He thought something must be wrong Jason was sure of it

Finally, just before Jason was going to bed, he decided to try to reach Todd one more time The phone rang several times before Todd's father answered Jason asked, "May I speak to Todd"

"I'm sorry, Jason, Todd can't come to the phone He had an accident this morning He tripped over the dog and broke his leg I think he may be back in school by Wednesday"

"Oh, I'm sorry to hear about his accident Would it be all right if I come by after school tomorrow"

"I'm sure Todd would like to see you Could you bring his assignments with you Even though he isn't feeling too well now, I know he won't want to get too far behind in his work"

"I'd be glad to do that Is there anything else I can do"

"No, I don't think so"

"All right Tell Todd I'll see him tomorrow Good night"

5. Read the letter carefully. Write in commas where they are needed.

235 Bridgewater Way
Lancaster Pennsylvania
April 22 199-

XYZ Company
1721 Baxter Street
Durham North Carolina 10456

Dear Sir:

Recently I purchased a skateboard manufactured by your company. I bought it at a local sports shop. The owner told me yours was the most popular skateboard in his store. He said "Rick I'm sure you will be pleased with this board. It is a strong durable board and I sell more of them than any other make."

Wanting the best board I bought it. However I did think $78.95 was a high price.

Last week I was using my new board to jump and turn in mid-air. Following the first jump one of the front wheels cracked. After this happened I examined the other wheels carefully. That was when I noticed that one of the back wheels had a crack.

I went back to the store. The owner was very nice but he said I would have to contact you directly about my problem.

I would like to have two sets of replacement wheels for my skateboard. One set would be for the front of the board and one set for the back. My skateboard is model #D6057E.

Thank you for your cooperation.

Yours truly
Rick Fowler

6. This passage needs a colon and semicolons. Read the story and put the punctuation where it belongs.

"You should be heading back to the permanent base at Little America your work here is done," said Richard Byrd in 1934. He said to his team members, "I'm disappointed we didn't reach the South Pole and we weren't able to transport enough supplies for two more people to stay here. But I'll be fine alone don't worry about me. You need to get back before the Antarctic winter sets in. It's already March 28 the winter will begin soon."

"Let's go over the supplies that are left," said one of the men. "You have the following food, water, cooking supplies, maps of the base camp and the route back to Little America, weather instruments, a radio, and emergency provisions."

7. This passage needs apostrophes and quotation marks. Read the passage and mark where the punctuation needs to go.

At last, after many months at sea, the lookout on Amerigo Vespuccis ship gave a joyful shout. He yelled, Land, ho! Amerigo and his crew felt theyd reached Asia at last.

Amerigo and several crew members got into the ships rowboat and rowed to shore. They were amazed at the surroundings they encountered. The jungles thickness spread down to the waters edge. Look at these trees, shouted several men.

Others asked, How will we ever be able to pass through here?

The men hadnt ever seen anything like this. One man asked, Where are Asias marble-bridged cities and great stores of riches?

Amerigo realized he hadnt reached Asia. He said to his men, Lets travel down the coast. Amerigo and his ships traveled 1,000 miles down the coastline. At each stop they found more jungles and a few native people. Nothing they saw fit Asias description.

One day, Amerigo exclaimed, This isnt Asia at all! I believe weve discovered a new continent!

Summary

In this unit, you have seen ways to revise and edit your writing. Do not be concerned about producing a perfect piece of writing. Professional writers and editors make mistakes when they write, too. After you have written your draft, go back over it and polish it. You may need to do this more than once.

Spelling and punctuation are important. However, do not let the mechanics of writing make you afraid to write! What you have to say is the most important part of writing.

Unit 4 Practice Revising and Editing

CHAPTER Six

Modeled Instruction

Many tests include exercises that test your revising and editing skills. Usually, you are given a writing sample filled with errors and asked multiple-choice questions about how the sample should be revised. In this chapter, you will find writing samples of the four types of writing: narrative, informational, persuasive/argumentative, and everyday. After each sample are multiple-choice questions such as the kind you would find on tests. We will provide you with strategies to help you answer these questions.

Narrative Text

Soccer has grown in popularity as a school and an organized league sport. It attracts both male and female players. Here is a story about a championship soccer game. Read the story and then answer the questions.

1   **The Most Exciting Day I Had**

2   The most exciting day I had was last month when we played Raritan
3   for the league soccer championship. My team, West, was undefeated, as
4   was Raritan. This was the last game of the season. Whoever won this
5   game would be the champions.

6   The game started fast. Both teams were well coached, fast, and
7   eager to win. The ball flied up and down the field. Being a center
8   striker, I took several shots on goal. But their goalie was almost always
9   in the right spot. She caught the ball each time and either threw or
10   punted it to one of her players'. I was only able to score once.

11   By the fourth quarter, the score was tied two all. But, after each
12   goal, Raritan tied the score. I was beginning to think the game might
13   end in a tie.

14   Suddenly, a penalty was called against West. Someone on my team
15   had triped a player by accident. The best kicker from Raritan went to
16   the line to take the penalty shot. About 200 people had bought tickets
17   to the game. The girl kicked the ball towards the corner of the net. Our
18   goalie dove for the ball. She caught it with her finger tips and fell to the
19   ground. We could still win the game.

20   When the ball game back into play, one of our halfbacks took
21   control of it and passed it to me at midfield. I started to dribble
22   toward Raritan's goal. One girl stood between me and the goal. Out
23   of the corner of my eye, I saw my friend Jean. I passed to her and
24   streaked toward the goal. She led me with a perfect pass in front of
25   the goal. I shot the ball to the far corner of the goal. Raritan's goalie
26   lunged toward the ball. She was too late. Just as the ball flew into the
27   net, the whistle blew ending the game.

28   I felt great! We had won the championship for the second year in a row!

1. What editing change, if any, is needed in lines 4-5 ("Whoever...champions.")?
   A. Change *whoever* to *whomever*.
   B. Change *won* to *one*.
   C. Change *would* to *will*.
   D. Make no change.

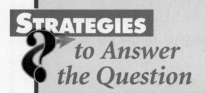

This question deals with different forms of words. Try to eliminate one or two choices that you know are wrong. This will narrow your focus. Remember, it is possible that it is correct as written.

2. What editing change is needed in line 7 ("The...field.")?
   A. Change *flied* to *flyed*.
   B. Change *flied* to *flies*.
   C. Change *flied* to *flew*.
   D. Change *flied* to *fly*.

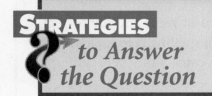

Decide which form of the verb is needed by trying the different forms in the sentence. You may be able to tell which one is correct by the way it sounds.

3. What editing change is needed in lines 9-10 ("She...players'.")?
   A. Change *caught* to *catch*.
   B. Change *threw* to *thrown*.
   C. Change *punted* to *punt*.
   D. Change *players'* to *players*.

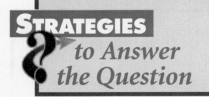

Try each of the changes suggested. See if one of them sounds correct. Watch for apostrophes; they are used to form a contraction or to show ownership.

4. How could you make the meaning clearer in lines 11-12 ("But...score.")?

   A. But Raritan tied the score again.

   B. After every goal we scored, Raritan tied the score.

   C. After each goal, Raritan tied the score.

   D. But, before each goal, Raritan tied the score.

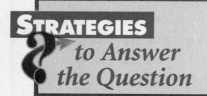

STRATEGIES to Answer the Question

Slip each sentence into the story. Which one makes the picture clearer for you? Think of the pace of the game and the closeness of the score.

5. What editing change, if any, is needed in lines 14-15 ("Someone...accident.")?

   A. Change *had* to *have*.

   B. Change *accident* to *acident*.

   C. Change *triped* to *tripped*.

   D. Make no change.

STRATEGIES to Answer the Question

You need to know the correct forms of verbs and the correct spelling of words. A good idea with spelling is to look at the word carefully. Your eyes can often catch a misspelling.

6. Which sentence can be omitted because it does NOT support the focus of paragraph 4?

   A. lines 15-16 ("The...shot.")

   B. lines 16-17 ("About...game.")

   C. line 17 ("The...net.")

   D. lines 18-19 ("She...ground.")

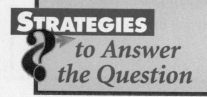

STRATEGIES to Answer the Question

Identify which sentence isn't needed in the paragraph.

7. Which editing change is needed in lines 20-21 ("When...midfield.") ?
  A. Change *ball* to *call*.
  B. Change *game* to *came*.
  C. Change *one* to *won*.
  D. Change *passed* to *past*.

This question requires you to proofread the sentence and look for an obvious spelling mistake.

8. What transition can be used at the beginning of the sentence in line 26 ("She...late.")?
  A. Therefore,
  B. Then,
  C. Furthermore,
  D. However,

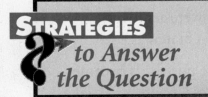

The transitional word should link the action in this sentence with the sentence before it.

Informational Text

When people travel, they like to send their family and friends postcards that show where they are. Here is an informational story that describes the development of the picture postcard. Read the text and then answer the questions that follow.

1	**The development of the Picture Postcard**
2	by John MacIntere

3 Picture postcards are found all over the world. People use these
4 small cards to show friends and relatives the sights from their trips.
5 Today, they are accepted as part of every tourist attraction. But there
6 was a time when they did not exist.

7 The first record of someone sending a picture postcard in the
8 United States was in 1862. While in the Union Army during the Civil
9 War, William Jackson sketched different activities happening around
10 camp. He sent these home with short messages on the back. This was
11 the prototype for what was to become the picture postcard.

12 In the years following the Civil War, Jackson traveled widely
13 throughout the United States. He photographed and drew many
14 sketches of the natural wonders he saw. These were sent with
15 inscriptions to people living all over the United States.

16 But it was not until almost 1900 that picture postcards became
17 available to everyone. In 1898, the United States Congress passed a
18 law allowing the mailing of picture postcards at the same rate as
19 government-made postcards. Picture postcards could be mailed
20 inexpensively. Second, an improved printing system was introduced
21 into the United States which allowed picture postcards to be made at
22 minimal cost. Almost anyone could afford picture postcards.
23 Travelers loved the cards. They could now send pictures of sights
24 they were enjoying to friends back home.

25 Today, picture postcards are a big business. Wherever you go, you
26 can purchase a picture postcard illustrating the local scene. People
27 usually buy postcards to send to friends, but some just keep them as
28 reminders of a trip, vacation, or visit.

9. What editing change, if any, is needed in line 1 ("The...Postcard.")?

A. Change *development* to *Development*.

B. Change *"The development of the Picture Postcard"* to *"The Development Of The Picture Postcard."*

C. Change *"The development of the Picture Postcard"* to *"The development of the picture postcard."*

D. Make no change.

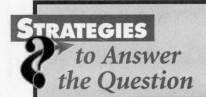

Think of the rules for capitalizing words in titles.

10. How should John revise the sentence in lines 3-4 ("People...trips.")?

A. These small cards allow people to show friends and relatives sights from their trips.

B. From their trips, people send friends and relatives sights.

C. Small cards showing the sights are sent by people to friends and relatives on trips.

D. People on trips send these small cards to their friends and relatives to show them sights from their trips.

Even if a sentence is written correctly, it can sometimes be improved so that it reads better. Read each choice and select the revision that makes the most sense.

11. What editing change, if any, is needed in line 5 ("Today. . . attraction.")?

    A. Change *they* to *postcards*.

    B. Change *accepted* to *excepted*.

    C. Change *tourist* to *tourist's*.

    D. Make no change.

STRATEGIES **to Answer the Question**

When you use pronouns, it must be clear which noun they are replacing. Here is an example: Carolyn brought some homemade cookies for her friends, but they were soon gone. The question is *what* was soon gone, the cookies or the friends? We assume it was the cookies, but it could have been the friends. If it is not clear to which noun the pronoun is referring, use the noun instead.

12. What revision is needed in lines 14-15 ("These. . . States.")?

    A. Then he wrote inscriptions for the sketches and sent them to people living all over the United States.

    B. These were sent with inscriptions, to various people, all over the United States.

    C. Inscriptions were written and sent to people all over the United States.

    D. People all over the United States were sent sketches with inscriptions.

STRATEGIES **to Answer the Question**

We need to have a clearer idea of what is being said in these lines. The revised sentence should contain all the main ideas from the original lines.

13. What transition is needed in lines 19-20 ("Picture...inexpensively.")?
   A. Later,
   B. Of course,
   C. As a result,
   D. Meanwhile,

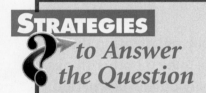

Look for a word that will connect two thoughts. Try each choice and see which best suits the situation.

14. What is the BEST revision for the sentences in lines 20-22 ("Second...postcards.")?
   A. Almost everyone can afford picture postcards in the United States.
   B. In addition an improved printing system made picture postcards available at a minimal cost, allowing almost anyone to afford them.
   C. In addition, an improved printing system, introduced in the United States, made picture postcards available at a minimal cost.
   D. Picture postcards were affordable at a minimal cost, allowing almost anyone to afford them, when a new printing system was introduced.

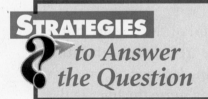

When you revise sentences, make sure you include all of the key points.

15. What editing change, if any, is needed in lines 26-28 ("People...visit.")?
   A Change *usually* to *usualy*.
   B. Change *buy* to *by*.
   C. Change *friends* to *friends'*.
   D. Make no change.

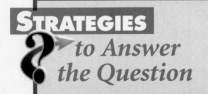

Think about spelling, homonyms, and plural or possessive forms of a word. Does the spelling seem correct? Is the correct word being used? Should the word be the plural possessive form? If not, then no change is needed.

Persuasive/Argumentative Text

Here is a letter that a student wrote to her school principal. She is concerned about the welfare of the students at her school. Read her letter and answer the questions that follow.

1   Dear Principal:

2   I have noticed that students have difficulty paying attention during
3   the last period of the day. Their attention seems to be on other things.
4   Also, students are tired and become restless easily during last period.
5   I have a solution to this problem. I would like you to consider it for
6   next year.

7   The last period could be an activity period for everyone. The
8   teachers could put together clubs. Based on their interests and on
9   student requests. Some of the many elective courses that are offered
10   could be run as clubs by the teachers. These would include art, music,
11   cooking, etc. Students could elect one activity course each marking
12   period. This would give students time to relax before going home.
13   In addition, students would enjoy theirselves more in these classes.
14   They would not need to worry about learning new concepts or writing
15   papers. They would use their energy and not have to sit still in a
16   classroom. They would no longer become restless at the end of the day.

17   In summary, I feel academic classes at the end of the day are not
18   productive. When students are tired, they have trouble concentrating
19   on difficult concepts. By having activities during last period, you can
20   improve learning. Students will be able to study more during the day
21   while looking forward to the activities at the end of the day.

22   Thank you for considering my suggestion.

23   Yours truly,

24   Jill Graham

16. What editing change, if any, is needed in the sentence in lines 2-3 ("I . . . day.")?

A. Change *students* to *student's*.

B. Change *difficulty* to *dificulty*.

C. Add a comma after *noticed*.

D. Make no change.

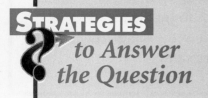

This question involves the skills of punctuation and spelling. Check the spelling first. If the words look correct, decide if the word *students* is plural or singular possessive. Is the letter speaking of a number of students, or of something owned by one student? Finally, is a comma needed here? If none of these changes are correct, then no change is needed.

17. What is the BEST way to combine the two sentences in lines 3-4 ("Their . . . period.")?

A. Because students are tired, they become restless and their attention seems to be on other things.

B. Their attention seems to be on other things, and students are tired and become restless easily during last period.

C. During last period, students are tired and restless, and their attention is on other things.

D. Tired and restless students' attention is on other things.

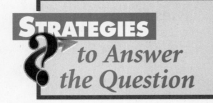

You need to combine the two sentences into one correct sentence. Choose the answer that contains information from both sentences and is worded clearly.

18. Which of these changes makes the meaning clearer in lines 5-6
("I would...year.")?

   A. Change *it* to *this problem*.

   B. Change *it* to *what I have in mind*.

   C. Add *using* after *consider*.

   D. Add *thinking about* before *it*.

STRATEGIES *to Answer the Question*

First decide what the word *it* stands for in the sentence. Next, reread the sentence with each of the suggested changes. See which one makes the sentence clearer.

19. Which is the BEST revision for the sentences in lines 7-9 ("The...requests.")?

   A. Clubs are based on their interests and on student requests.

   B. Teachers could put together clubs based on their interests and student requests.

   C. The teachers could put together clubs; based on their interest and student requests.

   D. Teachers could run interest clubs on request.

STRATEGIES *to Answer the Question*

One of these two sentences is really a fragment. It needs the information found in the sentence before it to make it a complete thought. Look for the choice that combines the two clearly.

20. What editing, if any, is needed in line 13 ("In...classes.")?

   A. Delete the comma after *In addition*.

   B. Change *students* to *students'*.

   C. Change *theirselves* to *themselves*.

   D. Make no change.

STRATEGIES *to Answer the Question*

This question involves the skills of punctuation and correct usage. Is the comma used correctly? Is the letter referring to a group of students, or is the reference to something the students own? Finally, is the word *theirselves* correct? If none of the choices are correct, then no change is needed.

21. What editing change, if any, is needed in lines 14-15 ("They...papers.")?
   A. Change *would* to *wood*.
   B. Change *new* to *knew*.
   C. Change *writing* to *write*.
   D. Make no change.

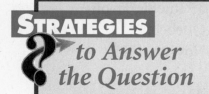

STRATEGIES
to Answer the Question

Two of these choices deal with homonyms. Is the correct word used in each case? Should the word *writing* be changed in this sentence? Is it possible that no correction is needed?

22. Which transition word is needed at the beginning of lines 19-20 ("By...learning.")?
   A. However,
   B. For example,
   C. Nevertheless,
   D. Consequently,

STRATEGIES
to Answer the Question

Each choice gives a different meaning to the sentence. Find the word that connects the ideas in this sentence with the sentence before it.

23. Which sentence BEST expresses Jill's viewpoint?
   A. Line 5 ("I...problem.")
   B. Lines 7-8 ("The...clubs.")
   C. Line 12 ("This...home.")
   D. Lines 17-18 ("In...productive.")

STRATEGIES
to Answer the Question

Look for the main idea expressed in the letter.

Everyday Text

Everyday texts include a wide assortment of materials. Here is a friendly letter, a common form of everyday text. The letter is written from one friend to another. Read the letter and answer the questions that follow.

1   35 Rue de Tivoli

2   Quebec, PQ D3N 8T4

3   Nov. 21, 1999

4   Dear Jacques,

5   Well, hear I am in school. Its much bigger than the one I went to
6   when I lived near you. It is harder to find my way around. There are
7   so many halls and the lockers are located all over the building. The
8   lockers are also tall, and I must stand on my toes to see the top shelf.
9   One good thing though, you can put alot of things in them because
10   everyone has his or her own locker. The kids are nice. They are all
11   friendly. Some have already helped me with my homework. I also
12   met someone who had moved here only three weeks ago. He is
13   helping me learn about the school and teachers.

14   Tomorrow we start basketball practice. In gym class, I saw most of
15   the kids who were on the team last year. I think I'll be able to make
16   the team. Hopefully, I will be able to play. The coach seems nice he
17   talked to me yesterday about the team. My courses are the same as
18   yours. I am taking literature, algebra, earth science, history, and
19   english. I am also taking technology and music. The band leader
20   wants me to try out for the band next week.

21   Write soon. I miss the other ninth graders back at champlain high
22   school. I hope everything is going well for you. Say hello to everyone
23   for me.

24   Your friend,

25   Marcel

24. What editing change, if any, is needed on line 5 ("Well...school.")?

    A. Remove the comma after *Well.*

    B. Change *school* to *School.*

    C. Change *hear* to *here.*

    D. Make no change.

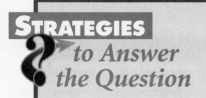

STRATEGIES *to Answer the Question*

This question involves the skills of capitalization, punctuation, and usage. First, decide if the comma is used correctly after the introductory word, *Well.* Then, see if the word *school* needs to be capitalized. Finally, decide which homonym is correct. If there are no errors, the answer is D.

25. What editing change, if any, is needed in lines 5-6 ("Its...you.")?

    A. Change *Its* to *It's.*

    B. Change *than* to *then.*

    C. Change *lived* to *live.*

    D. Make no change.

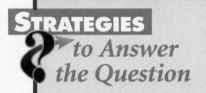

STRATEGIES *to Answer the Question*

This question involves the skills of punctuation, usage, and verb tense. In choice A, you must choose between the possessive form *Its* or the contraction *It's.* Choice B asks you to distinguish between the meaning of two words: *than* is used when comparing things; *then* is associated with a time sequence. Choice C refers to verb form. Choice D is correct if there are no changes needed.

26. What editing change, if any, is needed on lines 9-10 ("One...locker.")?

    A. Remove the comma after *though.*

    B. Change *alot* to *a lot.*

    C. Change *his* to *their.*

    D. Make no change.

STRATEGIES *to Answer the Question*

The skills involved in this question are punctuation, spelling, and correct usage. Before deleting or adding a comma, read the sentence both ways. Remember that a comma provides a pause in the sentence. Some words sound like a single word, though they are actually two words. Watch your agreement when using pronouns.

27. How could Marcel have combined the sentences on lines 10-11 ("The...homework.")?

    A. The kids are nice and friendly.

    B. The kids are nice and friendly, and some have helped me with my homework.

    C. The kids are nice, and they are friendly, and some have already helped me with my homework.

    D. The kids are nice and friendly because they help me with my homework.

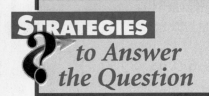

STRATEGIES *to Answer the Question*

Combine ideas into one well-constructed sentence. Select the choice that includes most of the important points from the three sentences.

28. What editing change, if any, should Marcel make in lines 16-17 ("The...team.")?

    A. Add a semicolon after *nice*.

    B. Add a colon after *nice*.

    C. Add a comma after *nice*.

    D. Make no change.

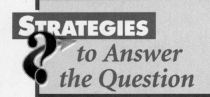

STRATEGIES *to Answer the Question*

When inserting punctuation, think of when each kind would be used. Then, decide which one is needed in this sentence.

29. What editing change, if any, should be made on lines 18-19 ("I...english.")?

    A. Change *english* to *English*.

    B. Change *earth science* to *Earth Science*.

    C. Change *algebra* and *history* to *Algebra* and *History*.

    D. Make no change.

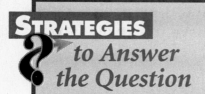

Think of the type of words that must be capitalized.

30. What editing change, if any, should be made on lines 21-22 ("Write...school.")?

    A. Change *champlain high school* to *Champlain high school*.

    B. Change *champlain high school* to *Champlain High School*.

    C. Change *graders* to *graders'*.

    D. Change *graders* to *grader's*.

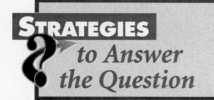

Decide if you need to capitalize any of the words in the name of the school. The other choices involve forming plural and possessive forms.

31. What editing change, if any, should Marcel make in the last sentence of his letter, lines 22-23 ("Say...me.")?

    A. Add a comma after *everyone*.

    B. Add a comma after *Say*.

    C. Add a comma after *Say*, and place quote marks before and after *hello*.

    D. Make no change.

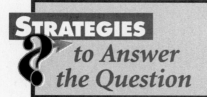

Use a comma only if it makes the meaning of the sentence clearer.

CHAPTER *Seven*

Guided Practice

In this chapter, you will read selections from each of the four types of writing. After each selection, there will be questions for you to answer. In addition to answering each question, you will have to explain why you made the choice that you did.

Narrative Text

Jim wrote this story describing how his family planned a recent trip. Read this story and then answer the questions that follow.

1   **Family Trip to Washington**

2   Have you ever gone to Washington D.C.? My dad came home last
3   night and said, "I think we should go to Washington for our next
4   vacation." This took everyone by surprise, because we had all talked
5   about going hiking in the Adirondack Mountains. However, after some
6   discussion, we all agreed it would be fun to see the United States capital.

7   My sister let us know what she wanted to see. She said, "I want to
8   go to the National Museum of American History. I've heard they have
9   a nice exhibit on the first ladies' gowns."

10   I agreed saying, "I want to go there, too, and see the exhibits on the
11   civil War." I also mentioned the Air and Space Museum would be fun
12   to visit.

13   Dad said, "We should be able to see both museums. Both are
14   worth visiting."

15   Each of us made a number of other suggestions. After discussing
16   them at some length, we decided to see as many sights as we could
17   in the three days we would be in Washington, D.C. Our list included
18   the following the two museums, the Tomb of the Unknown Soldier,
19   the White House, the Capitol, the Old Post Office, the FBI building,
20   the Lincoln Memorial, and the Vietnam War Memorial.

21   Of course getting to Washington would be half the fun. Dad
22   suggested we take the Metroliner and stay in a hotel near Union
23   terminal. I thought it would be fun to fly into National Airport,
24   but the train won out.

25   By the end of our planning, I was looking forward to touring
26   Washington. As Mom said, "The suggestion to go to Washington was
27   a surprise. Now that I've gotten used to it, I'm looking forward to the
28   adventure of seeing the sights of our capital."

1. What editing change is needed in line 2 ("Have...D.C.?")?
   A. Change *gone* to *went.*
   B. Change *D.C.* to *DC.*
   C. Add a comma after *Washington.*
   D. Change *ever* to *never.*

The answer is _____

Reason for choice _____

_____

2. What editing change, if any, is needed in lines 8-9 ("I've...gowns.")?
   A. Change *I've* to *"I've.*
   B. Change *exhibit* to *exibit.*
   C. Change *first ladies'* to *First Ladies'*
   D. Make no change.

The answer is _____

Reason for choice _____

_____

3. What editing change, if any, is needed in lines 10-11 ("I...War.")?
   A. Delete the comma after *saying.*
   B. Change the comma after *too* to a semicolon.
   C. Change *civil* to *Civil.*
   D. Make no change.

The answer is _____

Reason for choice _____

_____

4. What editing change, if any, is needed in lines 17-20 ("Our...Memorial.")?
A. Add a colon after *following*.
B. Change the commas to semicolons.
C. Put quote marks before *Our* and after *list*.
D. Make no change.

The answer is _____

Reason for choice _____

_____

5. What editing change, if any, is needed in lines 21-23 ("Dad...terminal.")?
A. Add a comma after *suggested*.
B. Change *Metroliner* to *metroliner*.
C. Change *Union terminal* to *Union Terminal*.
D. Make no change.

The answer is _____

Reason for choice _____

_____

6. What transition could be used before the sentence that starts on line 27 ("Now...capital.")?
A. Therefore,
B. Since,
C. However,
D. Consequently,

The answer is _____

Reason for choice _____

_____

7. Which sentence should be omitted because it does NOT support the focus of the story?
   A. line 2 ("Have...D.C.?")
   B. line 7 ("My...see.")
   C. line 15 ("Each...suggestions.")
   D. line 21 ("Of...fun.")

The answer is _____

Reason for choice _____

_____

8. What sentence BEST states the main idea of the story?
   A. line 2 ("Have...Washington D.C.?")
   B. lines 5-6 ("However...capital.")
   C. line 15 ("Each...suggestions.")
   D. line 21 ("Of...fun.")

The answer is _____

Reason for choice _____

_____

Informational Text

Carlos Ramirez was asked by his science teacher to research some aspect of modern technology and write a report about his findings. Read Carlos' report and answer the questions that follow.

1	**Computer Viruses: The Unwanted Bug**
2	by Carlos Ramirez

3　　Computer viruses are a rapidly growing problem in the computer
4　industry. They work by duplicating and attaching themselves to
5　programs installed on computers. Continual multiplying, they can cause
6　major problems in the operation of the software on any computer. Once
7　inside a computer, a virus attaches itself to the computer's operating
8　system. Here it duplicates itself. Then the virus attaches itself to other
9　programs that are installed. The virus is very contagious, able to
10　reproduce when turned on after being off for many hours.

11　　Unfortunately, computer viruses do not have any visible signs. You
12　will not know you have one until you start to notice the damage it
13　causes. The harm the virus does can vary, from using up available
14　memory to actually destroying data.

15　　Computer viruses are man-made; they do not occur naturally in
16　the computer. The first virus was identified in 1973. It wasn't until
17　1986 that a virus attached itself to a major commercial program. By
18　1988, a national computer organization identified nearly 90,000
19　different viruses.

20　　There's no foolproof way to protect a computer against a virus.
21　There are antiviral programs on the market. However, they are only
22　effective against the most common viruses. Many of the less
23　common viruses will bypass these programs.

24　　Computer owners can reduce their risk of "catching" a virus by
25　carefully monitoring the programs and any disks they use. Make
26　back-up copies of every important file. If a virus does attack, at least
27　your files will be safe.

9. What editing change, if any, is needed in lines 4-5 ("They…computers.")?
   A. Change *duplicating* to *duplicateing*.
   B. Change *attaching* to *ataching*.
   C. Change *itself* to *themselves*.
   D. Make no change.

The answer is _____

Reason for choice _____

_____

10. What editing change, if any, is needed in lines 5-6 ("Continual…computer.")?
   A. Change *Continual* to *Continually*.
   B. Change *multiplying* to *multiplied*.
   C. Change *cause* to *caused*.
   D. Make no change.

The answer is _____

Reason for choice _____

_____

11. What is the BEST revision for lines 9-10 ("The…hours.")?
   A. These viruses are very contagious; able to reproduce when a computer is turned on after many hours.
   B. The virus is very contagious, able to reproduce when a computer is turned on after being off for many hours.
   C. When a computer is turned on, viruses reproduce.
   D. Computer viruses are contagious for many hours.

The answer is _____

Reason for choice _____

_____

12. What would be a good transition word for the sentence starting on line 16 ("It…program.")?

A. Moreover,

B. Instead,

C. Likewise,

D. However,

The answer is _____

Reason for choice _____

_____

13. What is the BEST way for Carlos to combine the three sentences on lines 21-23 ("There…programs.")?

A. There are antiviral programs but they only work on some kinds of viruses.

B. Antiviral programs are on the market, and effective against common viruses.

C. Antiviral programs are effective against the most common viruses, but many less common ones will bypass these programs.

D. Antiviral programs are bypassed by uncommon viruses.

The answer is _____

Reason for choice _____

_____

14. What sentence BEST states the main idea of the article?

A. lines 3-4 ("Computer…industry.")

B. lines 6-8 ("Once…system.")

C. line 15-16 ("Computer…computer.")

D. lines 24-25 ("Computer…use.")

The answer is _____

Reason for choice _____

_____

Persuasive/Argumentative Text

In this section, you will read a letter that Wei Tseng wrote to the editor of a local newspaper. Wei was upset about something that the newspaper printed about his school. He presents his feelings in the letter.

1   Dear Editor:

2   As president of the student council at Terrence School, I am
3   writing in response to your editorial about the students at my school.
4   It was very unfair. It gave the wrong impression about how students
5   act in the halls and in class.

6   There is good discipline in our school. The students stay in their
7   seats in class. They listen to and respect all their teachers. In addition,
8   most students complete their homework assignments, which are
9   checked each day in class.

10   Yes we have some students who are always getting into trouble
11   with the teachers and principal. But in your editorial, you focused on
12   this very small number and did not look at the fact that most of the
13   students are hard-workers. Also, a large number of us participate in
14   after-school activities. These are fun and help us to meet people.
15   They also take a lot of time so you don't have time to fool around
16   after school like your editorial said.

17   Many of us also do volunteer work after school when we are not
18   involved with other activities. I pick up papers in the parks for the
19   recreation department many of my friends do similar volunteer
20   work. This is another fact you did not mention in your editorial.

21   Some of the students have part-time jobs after school. Having a
22   job means you didn't have time to get into trouble. If you want to get
23   good grades, you spend the time after work doing homework.

24   What bothers us most about your editorial is that apparently you
25   wrote it without even visiting our school. If you had come to our
26   school, you would have seen the things I mentioned in this letter.
27   You would have seen that we have very few discipline problems.
28   Then, you would not have written the editorial on discipline at
29   Terrence School.

30   Yours truly,

31   Wei Tseng, President
32   Student Council

15. What editing changes, if any, are needed in lines 4-5 ("It gave...class.")?
   A. Change *impression* to *impresion*.
   B. Change *students* to *students'*.
   C. Change *it* to *Your editorial*.
   D. Make no change.

The answer is _____

Reason for choice _____
_____

16. What is the BEST way to combine the two sentences in lines 6-7 ("The...teachers.")?

    A. The students stay in their seats in class; they listen to and respect their teachers.

    B. The students stay in their seats and they listen to their teachers and they respect their teachers.

    C. Students stay in their seats as they listen to their teachers and they respect their teachers.

    D. Students stay in their seats and listen to their teachers when they respect them.

The answer is _____

Reason for choice _____

_____

17. What editing change, if any, is needed in lines 10-11 ("Yes...principal.")?

    A. Add a comma after *Yes.*

    B. Add a comma after *students* and a comma after *trouble.*

    C. Add a comma after *trouble.*

    D. Make no change.

The answer is _____

Reason for choice _____

_____

18. What is the BEST way to revise lines 15-16 ("They...said.")?

    A. Besides these activities take a lot of time and we don't fool around, as indicated in your editorial.

    B. These activities leave us little time to fool around after school, as indicated in your editorial.

    C. We have little time to fool around after school, as indicated in your editorial.

    D. This leaves us little time to fool around, as indicated in your editorial.

The answer is _____

Reason for choice _____

_____

19. Which sentence does NOT support the focus of **paragraph 3, lines 10-16?**

    A. Lines 10-11 ("Yes...principal.")

    B. Lines 11-13 ("But...hard-workers.")

    C. Lines 13-14 ("Also...activities.")

    D. Line 14 ("These...people.")

The answer is _____

Reason for choice _____

_____

20. What revision is needed in lines 18-20 ("I...work.")?

    A. Put a comma after *papers.*

    B. Put a period after *papers* and capitalize the "*i*" in *in.*

    C. Put a comma after *parks.*

    D. Put a period after *department* and capitalize the "m" in *many.*

The answer is _____

Reason for choice _____

_____

21. What editing change should Wei make in the sentence in lines 21-22 ("Having...trouble.")?

    A. Change *didn't* to *can't.*

    B. Change *didn't* to *don't.*

    C. Change *have* to *had.*

    D. Change *have* to *has.*

The answer is _____

Reason for choice _____

_____

22. What is the BEST way to combine the three sentences in lines 25-27 ("If...problems.")?

    A. If you had come to our school, you would have seen that we have few discipline problems.

    B. If you had seen the things I mentioned in the letter, you would have seen that we have very few discipline problems.

    C. You would have seen that our discipline problems aren't like those you printed in your editorial, if you had come to our school.

    D. If you would have come to the school and seen all of the things I said in this letter, you would have seen that we don't have the discipline problems in the school like you said.

The answer is _____

Reason for choice _____

_____

Everyday Text

There are many forms of everyday texts. This one is a letter to an advice columnist. The writer has a problem and is seeking help.

1   Dear Problem Solver,

2   Recently, my parents have started to check up on me. They ask me
3   constantly "Have you done your homework? Who are you seeing?
4   When will you be home." It seems they have gotten more involved in
5   my life in the last month. I find it unbearable.

6   It all started when I brang Felipe home from school. I know a lot
7   of people think Felipe is a troublemaker. He's been caught cutting
8   class several times, and he does not do his homework all the time. He
9   is a good friend of mine. Many times he has helped me find
10 shortcuts for class assignments. Sometimes, hes even alerted me that
11 the teacher was going to give a test.

12   I like Felipe. He is fair and honest with me. Whenever I ask him a
13 question, he gives me a straight answer. Yes, I know he doesn't always
14 do his homework. But is that any reason why I shouldn't be his
15 friend? No! I still do my homework, and my grades are good.

16   My parents have started asking me all sorts of questions. They ask
17 where did I go, why were you five minutes late getting home, who
18 were you with? What's a guy to do?

19   Please help. I need a way to get my parents to stop asking so many
20 questions and to keep Felipe as a friend.

21   Signed,

22   Having Problems, Need Solutions

23. What change, if any, is needed in lines 2-3 ("They...homework?")?

    A. Change *ask* to *asked.*

    B. Add a comma after *constantly.*

    C. Change *Have* to *have.*

    D. Make no change.

The answer is _____

Reason for choice _____

_____

24. What change, if any, is needed in line 4 ("When...home?")?

    A. Add a comma after *When.*

    B. Change the period to a comma.

    C. Change the period to a question mark.

    D. Make no change.

The answer is _____

Reason for choice _____

_____

25. What revision, if any, is needed in line 6 ("It...school.")?

    A. Change *started* to *start.*

    B. Change *brang* to *brought.*

    C. Add a comma after *home.*

    D. Make no change.

The answer is _____

Reason for choice _____

_____

26. What transition is needed at the beginning of the sentence in lines 8-9 ("He...mine.")?
   A. Therefore,
   B. Sometimes,
   C. Moreover,
   D. However,

The answer is _____

Reason for choice _____

_____

27. What change, if any, is needed in lines 10-11 ("Sometimes...test.")?
   A. Delete the comma after *Sometimes*.
   B. Change *hes* to *he's*.
   C. Change *was* to *is*.
   D. Make no change.

The answer is _____

Reason for choice _____

_____

28. How should the writer revise the sentence in lines 16-18 ("They...with?")?
   A. They ask me where I go, whom I'm with, and why I'm late getting home.
   B. They ask where I go, whom I was with, and why was I late.
   C. They asks: where I went, whom I was with, and why I was late.
   D. They ask me: where I go, whom I with, and why was I late getting home.

The answer is _____

Reason for choice _____

_____

29. Which sentence BEST states the main idea of the letter?

    A. Lines 4-5 ("It...month.")

    B. Line 6 ("It...school.")

    C. Line 16 ("My...questions.")

    D. Lines 19-20 ("I...friend.")

The answer is _____

Reason for choice _____

_____

CHAPTER *Eight*
Independent Practice

In this chapter, you will read the four types of written texts and answer multiple-choice questions. However, you will not be given any strategies to help you, nor will you be asked any questions about your choice of answer. This is similar to what you could expect to find on a writing test.

Passage A

Here is a story about bravery. Read it carefully. Improve the organization, revise the sentence structure, and correct the mechanics.

1   **Braver than you Think**

2   Jacqueline always thought a person either was brave or wasnt. She
3   knew she was one of those people who certainly was not brave. She
4   was squeamish about handling worms. She was also extremely afraid of
5   snakes. She could tolerate viewing them behind thick glass walls in the
6   zoo. Jacqueline shuddered when she recalled a story her mother told
7   her involving her friends daughter, Rachel, and a snake.

8   One day, while on a camping trip in the Rocky Mountains. Rachel
9   was bitten by a snake. Her parents knew the snake was not venomous,
10   so they knew Rachel wasn't about to die. Try as they would, they
11   could not get the snake to release its grip on Rachel's thumb. It
12   seemed the snake had no intention of loosing its prey.

13   In desperation, the family drove Rachel and the tenacious snake to
14   the nearest hospital. Needless to say, the hospital emergency room
15   wasn't exactly prepared for this situation. Most snakebite victims
16   don't arrive with their attacker still firmly in toe. A few hasty calls
17   were made to different agencies to confirm that the reptile was
18   harmless. Only then did they proceed to pry the snake's jaws open
19   and release Rachel's thumb.

20   With Rachel's thumb swabbed and bandaged, the family left the
21   hospital to resume their camping holiday. The fate of the snake
22   is uncertain.

23   Thinking about this incident made Jacqueline cringe. She
24   wondered if she could show Rachel's kind of bravery in a situation
25   that frightened her. She hoped that she could, but she was in no
26   hurry to find out.

1. In the title, what change, if any, is needed ("Braver...Think")?

   A. Change *Think* to *think*.
   B. Change *than* to *then*.
   C. Change *than you* to *Than You*.
   D. Make no change.

2. What editing change is needed in line 2 ("Jacqueline...wasnt.")?

   A. Add a comma after *Jacqueline*.
   B. Change *always* to *all ways*.
   C. Add a comma after *brave*.
   D. Change *wasnt* to *wasn't*.

3. What transition is best in lines 5-6 ("She...zoo.")?

   A. However,
   B. Finally,
   C. In fact,
   D. Besides,

4. What change, if any, is needed in lines 6-7 ("Jacqueline...snake.")?

   A. Change *recalled* to *recall*.
   B. Change *friends* to *friend's*.
   C. Change *mother* to *Mother*.
   D. Make no change.

5. What is the BEST way to combine the sentences in lines 8-9 ("One...snake.")?

   A. One day on a trip Rachel was bitten by a snake.
   B. A snake bit Rachel in the Rocky Mountains.
   C. While on a camping trip, Rachel got bitten.
   D. While on a Rocky Mountain camping trip, Rachel was bitten by a snake.

6. What editing, if any, is needed in lines 10-12 ("Try…prey.")?

    A. Delete the comma after *would*.

    B. Change *loosing* to *losing*.

    C. Change *prey* to *pray*.

    D. Make no change.

7. What change, if any, is needed in lines 14-15 ("Needless…situation.")?

    A. Delete the comma after *say*.

    B. Change *hospital emergency room* to *Hospital Emergency Room*.

    C. Add a comma after *prepared*.

    D. Make no change.

8. What change, if any, is needed in lines 15-16 ("Most…toe.")?

    A. Add a comma after *Most*.

    B. Change *victims* to *victims'*.

    C. Change *toe* to *tow*.

    D. Make no change.

Passage B

Leary wrote the following book report for his social studies class. Read the report carefully. Improve the organization, revise the sentence structure, and correct the mechanics.

1   *The Mystery of the Bermuda Triangle*

2   by Leary Carrington

3   Almost all have heard about the Bermuda Triangle. What is it, and

4 is it as dangerous as the legend suggests. The author of *The Mystery*

5 *of the Bermuda Triangle* tells how it was named and weather it's as

6 dangerous as people say.

7   The Mystery of the Bermuda Triangle is a fast-reading, fact-filled

8 account of the mysterious events that have occurred in the region. The

9 book starts with a description of five war planes that were lost in 1945

10 and then tells about other famous losses. Included are how many of

11 the losses might have occurred. There are descriptions of the ocean

12 currents and weather patterns. The author makes the point that with

13 our increased scientific knowledge, we can now explain many of the

14 mysteries. When you study the meteorology and oceanography of the

15 part of the Atlantic Ocean in which the Bermuda Triangle is found,

16 you can account for most of the losses.

18   *The Mystery of the Bermuda Triangle* is an exciting book. It includes

19 mystery and suspense. While there is a lot of information in the

20 book. It is organized in a readable and understandable way. I would

21 recommend this book to anyone who is interested in learning about

22 the Bermuda Triangle.

9. What is the BEST revision for line 3 ("Almost...Triangle.")?

A. Almost all has heard of the Bermuda Triangle.

B. Almost all people have heard about the Bermuda Triangle.

C. All have heard about the Bermuda Triangle.

D. Almost everyone has heard about the Bermuda Triangle.

10. What editing change, if any, should Leary make in lines 3-4 ("What...suggests.")?

   A. Omit the comma after _What is it_.
   B. Add a question mark after _What is it_ and capitalize _and_.
   C. Add a semicolon after _What is it_.
   D. Change the period to a question mark.

11. What editing change, if any, is needed in lines 4-6 ("The...say.")?

   A. Change _tells_ to _tell's_.
   B. Change _it's_ to _its_.
   C. Change _weather_ to _whether_.
   D. Make no change.

12. What editing change, if any, is needed in lines 7-8 ("The...region.")?

   A. Omit the comma after _reading_.
   B. Italicize The Mystery of the Bermuda Triangle.
   C. Change _account_ to _acount_.
   D. Change _occurred_ to _ocurred_.

13. What is the BEST way for Leary to revise the sentences in lines 8-10 ("The...losses.")?

   A. The book begins with a description of the disappearance of five war planes in 1945, followed by accounts of other famous losses.
   B. The book starts with planes lost in 1945 and other losses.
   C. The book tells of mysterious disappearances in the region, beginning with five war planes lost in 1945.
   D. The book starts with a description of the war planes lost in 1945 and then covers some other famous losses.

14. What changes, if any, should be made in lines 10-12 ("Included...occurred.") to clarify the meaning?

    A. After *Included* add *in the book.*

    B. Change *Included are* to *It goes on to explain.*

    C. After *losses* add *of the war planes.*

    D. Make no change.

15. Where in paragraph 2 would it be BEST to place the sentence in lines 14-16 ("When...losses.")?

    A. after line 8 ("...region.")

    B. after line 10 ("...losses.")

    C. after line 12 ("...patterns.")

    D. where it is

16. How would you revise the sentences in lines 19-20 ("While...way.")?

    A. While there is a lot of information in the book, it is organized in a readable and understandable way.

    B. It is organized in a readable and understandable way, while there is a lot of information in the book.

    C. A lot of the information in the book is organized in a readable and understandable way.

    D. However, there is a lot of information in the book that is readable and understandable.

Passage C

Jill wrote the following letter to the principal about closing school because of a storm. Read the letter carefully. Improve the organization, revise the sentence structure, and correct the mechanics.

1   January 10, 1999

2   Dear Mr. Panos:

3   I am writing to complain about the closing of school yesterday
4   because of snow. I arrived at school only to find it was closed. I left
5   home for school at 7:50 A.M. At that time, the local radio station did
6   not list our school as being closed.

7   There certainly was enough snow on the ground when I left my
8   house yesterday morning. There must have been almost eight inches of
9   snow on the ground and it was still snowing. No one had shoveled the
10   sidewalk yet. And it was tough walking. The snow was higher than my
11   boots in most spots. Also I couldn't see the curbs. I almost fell twice.

12   I find it hard to understand why school wasn't closed earlier. In
13   science class, our weather station predicted snow the day before. All
14   the news stations were predicting more than a foot of snow last
15   night. Everyone knew it was coming.

16   I am sure our science teacher would be happy to share our class's
17   weather predictions with you if it would help you make a decision
18   about closing school. Also, I would be willing to get up early in the
19   morning to check the streets in my neighborhood if that would help.

20   Please let me know if you would like to receive our daily weather
21   prediction for the remainder of this winter.

22   Yours truly,

23   Jill Montel

17. What word inserted before *closing* in line 3 would make the sentence more logical?

   A. late
   B. later
   C. lateness
   D. lately

18. Which words should Jill add after *ground* in line 7 to clarify the meaning of the sentence?

   A. to close the school
   B. to fall
   C. to build a winter wonderland
   D. to open the school

19. What editing change, if any, is needed in lines 8-9 ("There…snowing.")?

   A. Add a comma after *snow*.
   B. Add a comma after *snow* and after *ground*.
   C. Add a comma after *ground*.
   D. Make no change.

20. What is the BEST way for Jill to combine the three sentences in lines 9-11 ("No one…spots.")?

   A. In spots, the snow on the unshoveled sidewalks was higher than my boots, making walking difficult.
   B. No one had shoveled the sidewalks yet, and it was tough walking in snow that was higher than my boots in some spots.
   C. The snow was higher than my boots in some spots, and yet, no one had shoveled the sidewalks; and it was difficult walking.
   D. Higher than my boots, the snow was in some spots, and yet, no one shoveled the sidewalks.

21. What is the BEST revision of lines 12-13 ("In...before.")?

    A. Our school has a weather station that predicts snow.

    B. The weather station, the day before, in our science class predicted snow.

    C. Our science class predicts snow using our weather station.

    D. The day before, the weather station in our science class predicted snow.

22. Which transitional word would make line 15 clearer ("Everyone...coming.")?

    A. Nevertheless,

    B. However,

    C. So,

    D. But,

23. What editing change, if any, is needed in lines 16-18 ("I...school.")?

    A. Change *science* to *Science*.

    B. Add a comma after *you*.

    C. Add a semicolon after *help*.

    D. Make no change.

24. Which sentence BEST states the main idea of Jill's letter?

    A. Lines 3-4 ("I...snow.")

    B. Lines 7-8 ("There...morning.")

    C. Lines 12-13 ("In...before.")

    D. Lines 16-18 ("I...school.")

Passage D

Someone with a problem wrote the following letter to an advice columnist. Read the letter carefully. Improve the organization, revise the sentence structure, and correct the mechanics.

1   Dear Dolores,

2   I need some advice. How do you deal with a mother that wants
3   you to take your little brother everywhere you go?

4   As you can imagine Mom thinks I should take my brother everywhere
5   I go. Whenever I go out, I'm asked to take Jamal along. It's gotten so bad,
6   I don't want to tell my mom I am going out to meet my friends.

7   Please understand, Jamal is a good kid. He is polite, funny, and
8   listens to what I tell him. The problem is that he is only eight years
9   old. I am the laughing stock of my friends.

10   Just last week, a group of us were planning to go to the shopping
11   mall. As I was going out the door, Mom asked me to take Jamal along.
12   I told her I didn't want to take him because it would interfere with
13   my shopping and meeting people. Mom said, "he is your brother and
14   won't be any trouble. He will just tag along."

15   When I met my friends, they kidded me saying, "What, baby-sitting
16   again"? I was so embarrassed.

17   What am I to do? I like my little brother, but enough is enough.
18   He has his own friends, and I have mine. Why must I be stuck taking
19   him along all the time?

20   Please tell me how I can get Mom to stop forcing me to watch my
21   little brother all the time.

22   Signed,

23   The Baby Brother Blues

25. What editing change, if any, is needed in lines 2-3 ("How...go?")?

  A. Change *mother* to *Mother*.

  B. Change *that* to *who*.

  C. Add a comma after *mother*.

  D. Make no change.

26. What editing change, if any, is needed in lines 4-5 ("As...go.")?

  A. Add a comma after *imagine*.

  B. Change *Mom* to *mom*.

  C. Change *go* to *went*.

  D. Make no change.

27. How would you revise the sentences in line 5 ("Whenever...along.") to make the paragraph more logical?

  A. I'm asked to take Jamal along.

  B. Whenever I go out, Jamal comes along.

  C. My mother asks me to take Jamal along whenever I go out with my friends.

  D. Whenever I go outside to be with my friends, I'm asked to take Jamal along.

28. What would clarify lines 7-8 ("He...him.")?

  A. Add *Jamal is* before *funny*.

  B. Change *polite* to *a polite boy*.

  C. Change *funny* to *has a funny sense of humor*.

  D. Change *listens to what I tell him* to *well-behaved*.

29. Where is the BEST place to move the sentence in line 9 ("I...friends.")?

  A. after line 3

  B. after line 6

  C. after line 16

  D. after line 21

30. What editing change, if any, is needed in the sentence in lines 13-14 ("Mom...trouble.")?

   A. Change *he* to *He*.
   B. Change *won't* to *wont*.
   C. Change *brother* to *Brother*.
   D. Make no change.

31. What editing change, if any, is needed in lines 15-16 ("When...again"?)?

   A. Delete the comma after *friends*.
   B. Change *kidded* to *kided*.
   C. Change *again"?* to *again?"*
   D. Make no change.

32. What is the purpose of the letter?

   A. Lines 2-3 ("I...go.")
   B. Line 9 ("I...friends.")
   C. Lines 15-16 ("When...again"?)
   D. Lines 20-21 ("Please...time.")

Unit 5 Practice Tests

Practice Test A

Directions for Writing Practice Test A, Part A1

This is Part 1 of the Writing Test. This part consists of a task in which you will be expected to show how well you can write. For this exercise, you are asked to complete the writing task below.

Take the time to think about the writing task and how you will organize what you want to say before you begin to write. Make any outline, notes, lists, organizers, etc. you wish. Your prewriting will not be scored. Only your writing will be scored. Do your best to make your writing clear and well-organized. Keep in mind the purpose of your writing task as well as your audience.

You may not use a dictionary or any other reference materials during the test. However, you may use the "Writer's Checklist" on page 144, which lists important points for you to remember as you write. If you finish early, go back over your writing using the "Writer's Checklist" to read critically and improve what you have written.

Do not go on to Part 2 until you receive further directions.

Writing Task

Writing Situation

Your school has just announced an essay contest. The person who writes the winning essay gets $100. The essay must be about what you would do with the $100 prize if you won it.

Directions for Writing

Write an essay for this contest. You will want to state what you plan to do with the $100 prize. Be specific about how you will spend the money and include reasons why you would spend it that way. Since you will be competing against many students, you will want to convince the judges why you should win.

Directions for Writing Practice Test A, Part A2

This is Part 2 of the Writing Test. This part consists of four passages in need of editing. Each passage is followed by multiple-choice questions related to the editing of the passage. Read the entire passage before answering the questions.

Passage A

Benjamin wrote this story for his English class. He would like you to look it over.

Read the story and help Benjamin improve his organization, revise his sentence structure, and correct his mechanics. Write in the text as you read, revise, and edit.

1   **Adventure on the Trail**

2   We must find the trail to our cabin soon, I thought. Nicolas and I had
3 been walking for at least two hours. "Nick, how long 'till we get to the
4 cabin?" I asked my friend, who claimed he knew where he was going.

5   "Well cross the trail to the cabin in five or ten minutes, Jim," he replied.

6   "Great," I mumbled to myself. About 30 minutes ago, he had told me
7 the trail was only a little further. He was lost and didn't want to admit it. I
8 wondered if our friends were worried about us. "Nick, I've got to stop," I
9 said. I sat down in the middle of the trail. Sudden, I heard sounds far off in
10 the woods, to the right side of the trail. Something was moving towards us.

11   "Nick," I whispered, "Do you hear what I hear?"

12   "What do you think it is?" he whispered back.

13   "I don't know," I said. "Maybe it's a bear. Whatever it is, it's moving
14 closer." We both started to walk quickly. Five minutes later, we stopped to
15 listen. The sounds were still behind us. We were scared. We started to run.
16 "I tripped over a stone and hit my knee on the ground," Nicolas said. "I
17 don't think I will be able to run or even walk." Just as we rounded a bend
18 in the trail, Nicolas let out a cry of pain.

19   "We've got to move," I said to him. "I don't have any desire to meet
20 whatever is behind us." I helped Nicolas get up. He put one arm around
21 my shoulders for support. We started to move slowly down the trail.

22   A voice called out. "Jim, Nick, am I glad I found you." I turned around
23 and stared. "Bill," I said. What are you doing here?"

24   "I was worried about you guys," Bill explained. Nicolas and I started to
25 laugh. "Why are you laughing?" asked Bill. "getting lost is no joke."

26   "We are not laughing at what you said," I gasped between laughs. "We
27 thought you were a bear."

1. What changes should Benjamin make in lines 3-5 ("Nick, how...replied.")?
   A. Change the question mark to a period following *cabin*.
   B. Change *Well* to *We'll*.
   C. Delete the comma after *minutes*.
   D. Put quotes after *replied*.

2. What changes, if any, should be made to lines 6-7 ("Great...admit it.")?
   A. Change *told* to *tells*.
   B. Change *trail was* to *trail were*.
   C. Change *didn't* to *doesn't*.
   D. Make no change.

3. What changes are needed to the sentences in lines 9-10 ("Sudden...us.")?
   A. Change *Sudden* to *Suddenly*.
   B. Delete the comma after *Sudden*.
   C. Put quotes in front of *I* and after *us*.
   D. Change *right* to *rite*.

4. What revisions should Benjamin make to combine the sentences in line 15 ("We were...run.") into one sentence?
   A. We were scared; we started to run.
   B. We were scared and we started to run.
   C. We started to run in fear.
   D. Since we were scared, we started to run.

5. Where is the BEST place for the sentences in lines 16-17 ("I tripped...or even walk.")?
   A. Line 18, after *cry of pain*.
   B. Line 19, after *said to him*.
   C. Line 20, after *is behind us."*
   D. Line 21, after *for support*.

6. Which transition is needed at the beginning of the sentence in line 22 ("A...out.")?
   A. Therefore,
   B. However,
   C. Softly,
   D. Suddenly,

7. What changes, if any, should be made to the sentences in lines 22-23 ("I turned...here?")?
   A. Change *stared* to *staired*.
   B. Move the question mark outside the quotes after *here*.
   C. Add a quote mark before *What*.
   D. Make no change.

8. What changes, if any should Benjamin make on line 25 ("Why...no joke.")?
   A. Change *getting* to *Getting*.
   B. Change the question mark to a comma.
   C. Change the period after Bill to a semicolon.
   D. Make no change.

GO ON

Passage B

Jamie wrote the following book report for her social studies class. She has asked you to look it over for her and help her correct it before she turns it in.

Read the report carefully and help her improve her organization, revise her sentence structure, and correct her mechanics. Feel free to write in the text as you read, revise, and edit the report.

1   ***Overland Stage***

2   *A Book Report by Jamie Jones*

3   Have you ever wondered what it felt like to ride in a stagecoach across the
4 frontier? What was life really like when riding in one of those coaches.

5   *Overland Stage* is a word and picture history of the red and gold
6 stagecoaches that rolled across the American West in the 1860s. The author
7 describes how the stagecoaches were made, what it was like riding in them,
8 and their importance in the settlement of the Old West.

9   The part of the book that was of most interest to me was a description
10 of an actual 19-day trip from Atchison, Kansas to Placerville, California.
11 The author details every day of the trip. The passengers never knew when
12 something might happen. It could be an exciting and dangerous trip.
13 Many days were long and boring. Surprisingly most stages were made
14 in Concord, New Hampshire.

15   Each stage weighed over a ton, stood eight feet tall, and left a track five
16 and a half feet wide. They were all painted. The body rested on leather
17 springs, making the ride unusually comfortable for that period of time.
18 Today, some of the origanal stages can be found in museums.

19   Pictures and drawings are an important part of this book. Each page
20 contains illustrations, which help the reader understand the authors
21 explanations.

22   This is a very informative book about an exciting but short-lived period
23 of American history. Less than ten years after the first stage crossed the
24 frontier, the main routes were being replaced by train tracks.

25   I would recommend this book to anyone interested in the history of the
26 American West.

9. What editing change, if any, should Jamie make in line 4 ("What...coaches.")?
   A. Change the period to a question mark.
   B. Add a comma after *like*.
   C. Add a question mark after *like* and change *when* to *When*.
   D. Make no change.

10. What editing change, if any, is needed in lines 5-6 ("*Overland*...1860s")?
    A. Change *Overland Stage* to Overland Stage.
    B. Change *history* to *History*.
    C. Change *American* to *american*.
    D. Make no change.

11. What editing change, if any, should Jamie make in the sentence in lines 6-8 ("The...West.")?
    A. Change *describes* to *describe*.
    B. Change *were* to *was*.
    C. Change *were* to *are*.
    D. Make no change.

12. How should Jamie combine the sentences in lines 12-13 ("It...boring.") into one sentence?
    A. It could be an exciting, dangerous, long, boring trip.
    B. The trip could be exciting and dangerous or long and boring.
    C. It could be an exciting and dangerous trip; many days were long and boring.
    D. It could be an exciting and dangerous trip, because many days were really long and boring.

13. What changes, if any, are needed in lines 13-14 ("Surprisingly...Hampshire.")?
    A. Add a comma after *Surprisingly*.
    B. Add a comma after *made*.
    C. Remove the comma after *Concord*.
    D. Make no change.

14. What would be a better location for the sentence in lines 13-14 ("Surprisingly...Hampshire.")?
    A. after line 6 ("...1860s.")
    B. before line 19
    C. after line 11("...trip.")
    D. after line 24

15. What editing change, if any, should Jamie make in the word "origanal" in line 18?
    A. original
    B. oreganal
    C. origanel
    D. Make no change.

16. How can Jamie make the sentence on lines 23-24 ("Less...tracks.") clearer?
    A. Replace *after the first stage crossed the frontier* with *ago*.
    B. Change *stage* to *stagecoach*.
    C. Add *stagecoach* before *routes*.
    D. Add *trains and* before *train tracks*.

GO ON

Passage C

Colette wrote this letter to the editor of the local newspaper to ask him to participate in a drug education project. She has asked you to help her improve it.

Read the letter carefully and help Colette improve her organization, revise her sentence structure, and correct her mechanics. Feel free to write in the text as you read, revise, and edit the letter.

1   June 5, 1999

2   Dear Editor:

3   I am writing to ask your support for Wynwood Middle School's drug
4 education project. Our school voted to sponsor a Drug Awareness Day
5 Parade on May 25.

6   We feel it is important that everyone in the community speak out against
7 drugs. After discussing the matter, we decided that having a parade down
8 main street was the best way to encourage everyone in the community to
9 come out against drugs. We plan to contact local stores to see if they will
10 sponsor such an event. With their support, we can purchase tee-shirts
11 saying, "Say No to Drugs" for all the marchers. We might even have enough
12 money left over to buy signs.

13   Our principal plans to speak to the superintendent to ask him if the
14 student's in all schools can march together. We would like students from each
15 grade to learn several songs to sing as they march down the street. Our
16 school band will lead the parade, which will end at the stadium. There
17 everyone will listen to speakers talk about drug abuse. If all the students in
18 the local schools participate, there will be over 2,000 students.

19   Would your newspaper publish original student writings on drugs and
20 drug use? Students at my school are researching the problems caused by
21 drugs and writing about what we find. If these articles were published, we
22 believe it would increase interest in the parade. The more people who
23 know about the parade, the more who will participate. We want to
24 encourage everyone in town to participate in our Drug Awareness Day.

25   If you are interested in suporting our project, we would be happy to
26 meet with you at Wynwood Middle School to discuss this.

27   Thank you for your consideration of our request.

28   Yours truly,

29   Colette Vernon, Student Council President

17. What is the BEST way for Colette to combine the two sentences in lines 3-5 ("I...May 25.")?
    A. Wynwood Middle School are sponsoring a Drug Awareness Day Parade on May 25, and we were wondering if you might give us your support?
    B. Wynwood Middle School is having a parade, and we need your support.
    C. Wynwood Middle School's drug education project is to sponsor a Drug Awareness Day Parade on May 25.
    D. I am writing to ask for your support for the May 25 Drug Awareness Day Parade, sponsored by Wynwood Middle School.

18. What editing change, if any, is needed in lines 7-9 ("After...drugs.")?
    A. Change the comma to a semicolon.
    B. Change *parade* to *Parade*.
    C. Change *main street* to *Main Street*.
    D. Make no change.

19. Which revision, if any, should Colette make in the sentence in lines 9-10 ("We...event.")?
    A. Change *We plan* to *We will plan*.
    B. Change *they will sponsor* to *they sponsor*.
    C. Change *they will* to *they are going to*.
    D. Make no change.

20. What editing change, if any, is needed in lines 13-14 ("Our...together.")?
    A. Change *principal* to *Principal*.
    B. Change *superintendent* to *Superintendent*.
    C. Change *student's* to *students*.
    D. Make no change.

21. Where would be the BEST place to move paragraph 4, lines 19-24 ("Would...Day.")?
    A. before paragraph 1
    B. after paragraph 1
    C. after paragraph 5
    D. Leave it where it is.

22. What would be the BEST way to revise the sentences in line 19-21 ("Would...find.")?
    A. Would you publish student articles based on research into problems caused by drug abuse?
    B. Would your newspaper publish articles that our teachers asked us to write after they had us do research into the problems that are caused by drugs?
    C. We want to know if your newspaper would publish the original writings our teachers asked us to do on drugs.
    D. Our teachers had us write original essays after we did research on the problems that are caused by drugs; and we would like your newspaper to publish them, if possible.

23. What editing change is needed in lines 25-26? ("If...this.")?
    A. Change *interested* to *interasted*.
    B. Change *interested* to *intarested*.
    C. Change *suporting* to *suportting*.
    D. Change *suporting* to *supporting*.

24. Which sentence BEST expresses the focus of the letter?
    A. Lines 7-9 ("After...drugs.")
    B. Lines 16-17 ("There...abuse.")
    C. Lines 20-21 ("Students...find.")
    D. Line 27 ("Thank...request.")

GO ON

Passage D

Jiro wrote a letter to invite his cousin Yuichi for the holiday weekend. Jiro's mother has suggested you look it over with him to make sure it is correct before he sends it.

Read the letter carefully and help Jiro improve his organization, revise his sentence structure, and correct his mechanics. Feel free to write in the text as you read, revise, and edit the letter.

1   April 28, 1999

2   Dear Yuichi,

3   I wanted to write and invite you to my house for the holiday weekend. I
4 checked with my parents, and they said it would be okay for you to come.

5   Bring your sleeping bag and pup tent so we can go camping one night.
6 There is a neat county park near my house. There are good campsites.
7 The trails are excellent. There is even a swimming pool. They also have a
8 lake where we can fish. I know you will enjoy it.

9   A new arcade in a mall. It's a short drive from my house. I have been
10 there three times since it opened. They have this great virtual realty game
11 for which you are a pilot in a star-fighter just like in *Star Wars*. I was able
12 to get the highest score on my third try. Maybe you will be able to get an
13 even higher score than I.

14   Do you want to play baseball on Monday? There's one thing I need
15 to know. We would need to play in the morning, as my father's company
16 picnic is in the afternoon. If you do want to play baseball, let me know
17 in your letter. I will ask the guys to get together then.

18   Well, I have to go now. Let me know if you can come over the long
19 holiday weekend. If you can, my parents will pick you up at the train
20 station on Friday evening.

21   Your cousin,

22   Jiro

25. What revision should Jiro make in the sentence in line 3 ("I...weekend.")?
 A. I want to invite you to my house for the holiday weekend.
 B. I wanted to write, and invite you to my house for the holiday weekend.
 C. I wanted to write and to invite you for the holiday weekend to my house.
 D. I am inviting you for the holiday weekend to my house.

26. What editing change, if any, should Jiro make in the sentence on lines 3-4 ("I...come.")?
 A. Change *parents* to *parents'*.
 B. Change *parents* to *parent's*.
 C. Change *parents* to *Parents*.
 D. Make no change.

27. How should Jiro combine the sentences on lines 6-8 ("There is a...fish.") into one sentence?
 A. There is a neat county park near my house with good campsites, and the trails are excellent, and there is even a swimming pool, and a lake where we can fish.
 B. The county park near my house has good campsites, excellent trails, a swimming pool, and a lake where we can fish.
 C. There is a county park near my house with good campsites, and with excellent trails and even with a swimming pool, and a lake where we can fish.
 D. A county park has campsites, trails, swimming, and fishing.

28. All of the following sentences support the focus of the third paragraph (lines 9-13) EXCEPT
 A. lines 9-10 ("I...opened.")
 B. lines 10-11 ("They...*Wars.*")
 C. lines 11-12 ("I...try.")
 D. lines 12-13 ("Maybe...I.")

29. How should Jiro revise the two sentences in line 9 ("A...house.")?
 A. There's a new arcade in a mall a short drive from my house.
 B. A new arcade a short drive away from my house opened.
 C. A new arcade from my house is only a short drive.
 D. Only a short drive from my house opened a new arcade.

30. What editing change, if any, should Jiro make in lines 10-11 ("They...*Wars.*")?
 A. Change *realty* to *reality*.
 B. Change *realty* to *reelty*.
 C. Change *realty* to *realety*.
 D. Make no change.

31. What change in organization would BEST improve the fourth paragraph (lines 14-17) of this letter?
 A. Move the third sentence ("We...afternoon.") to the beginning of the paragraph.
 B. Switch the first sentence ("Do...Monday?") with the second sentence ("There's...know.").
 C. Move the last sentence ("I...then.") after the third sentence ("We...afternoon").
 D. Move the fourth sentence ("If...letter.") to the beginning of the paragraph.

32. What editing change, if any, is needed in lines 18-19 ("Let...weekend.")?
 A. Add a comma after *know*.
 B. Add a comma after *know* and after *come*.
 C. Add a comma after *come*.
 D. Make no change.

133

Practice Test B

Directions for Writing Practice Test B, Part B1

This is Part 1 of the Writing Test. This part consists of a task in which you will be expected to show how well you can write. For this exercise, you are asked to complete the writing task on the next page.

Take the time to think about the writing task and how you will organize what you want to say before you begin to write. Make any outline, notes, lists, organizers, etc. you wish; your prewriting will not be scored. Only your writing will be scored. Do your best to make your writing clear and well-organized. Keep in mind the purpose of your writing task as well as your audience.

You may not use a dictionary or any other reference materials during the test. However, you may use the "Writer's Checklist" on page 144, which lists important points for you to remember as you write. If you finish early, go back over your writing using the "Writer's Checklist" to read critically and improve what you have written.

Do not go on to Part 2 until you receive further directions.

Writing Task

Writing Situation

Last week, someone broke into the local mall. Although nothing was stolen, plants were uprooted, benches were overturned, and some small booths and carts were damaged. One of your friends bragged to you that he and some other friends were the culprits.

This raises a question for you: Should you tell an adult when a friend of yours has done something illegal?

You decide to write an article for your school newspaper about this controversial question. Think about this issue and decide how you feel.

Directions for Writing

Write an article for your school newspaper expressing your point of view on the question of whether you should tell an adult when a friend of yours has done something illegal. Express your point of view clearly, and support it with reasons and evidence. Remember that some of your readers will have a different opinion; therefore, you should try to convince them with specific and logical reasons for your point of view.

Directions for Writing Practice Test B, Part B2

This is Part 2 of the Writing Test. This part consists of four passages in need of editing. Each passage is followed by multiple-choice questions related to the editing of the passage.

Read the entire passage before answering the questions. Mark only one answer for each test item.

Passage A

The following article was written by a high school journalism student who is an intern at her hometown newspaper near Washington, D.C. Before she hands the article in to her editor, she needs you to read the story and correct any errors in sentence structure, spelling, and punctuation, or to improve her organization where possible.

1   **A Lucky Kangaroo**

2   One hot May day in the National zoo in Washington, D.C., a mother
3   dumped her tiny three-month-old baby out of her pouch. Most baby
4   kangaroos, or joeys, are just beginning to peak out of the pouch at three
5   months. But for some unknown reason, this young mother was rejecting
6   her baby.

7   A zoo employee quickly picked up the six-inch baby and took him to
8   the zoo's clinic. The veterinarians doubted that the joey named Rufus
9   would live. Four women who worked at the zoo volunteered to take care
10 of him night and day. Rufus spent his days at the zoo but at night he went
11 home with one of the volunteers.

12   Rufus only weighed one and a half pounds when he was rejected by his
13 mother. He had to be fed baby formula every two hours. Jamie Bojan, one of
14 the volunteers, said, "Its a wonderful opportunity that I don't think any of us
15 would trade for anything. But oh, my gosh, it's been a lot of sleepness nights."

16   One of the most difficult parts of the job was attempting to provide
17 Rufus with a normal upbringing. Several times a day, one of the keepers
18 had to hold Rufus in a cloth pouch and jump around with him, imitating
19 the movements of a mother kangaroo. This movement is important to a
20 joey's development. Bojan says ",It felt very silly. We would do this little
21 rain dance, hopping around and then dipping to the left and right."

22   As Rufus became stronger, he turned into a playful youngster.
23 Whenever possible, he escaped from his covered playpen. He loved to hop
24 and kick and somersault. He made Theresa Cummings, one of the
25 volunteers, angry by chewing on her antique dining table. Theresa has
26 very valuable antiques at home.

27   When he's about a year and a half old, Rufus will be reunited with the
28 other kangaroos. In a short time, he probably won't even remember the
29 people who worked so hard to give him a chance to live.

1. What editing change, if any, should be made in line 2?
   A. Put a colon after *Washington*.
   B. Take the periods out of *D.C.*
   C. Capitalize the word *zoo*.
   D. Make no change.

2. What editing change, if any, should be made in lines 3-5 ("Most...months.")?
   A. Add an *e* before the *s* in *joeys*.
   B. Take out the comma after *kangaroos*.
   C. Make no change.
   D. Change *peak* to peek.

3. How could the sentences in lines 8-10 ("The...day.") be revised and combined?
   A. Take out the period after *live* and change *Four* to 4.
   B. Change the period after *live* to a semicolon.
   C. Change the period after *live* to a comma and then insert *but*.
   D. Make no change.

4. What punctuation is needed after the word *zoo* in line 10?
   A. semicolon
   B. colon
   C. no punctuation
   D. comma

5. What editing change, if any, is needed in lines 13-15 ("Jamie...anything.")?
   A. Change *Its* to *It's*.
   B. Change *Its* to *their*.
   C. Change *that* to *which*.
   D. Make no change.

6. What change, if any, is needed in line 15?
   A. Take out the comma after *oh*.
   B. Change *sleepness* to *sleepless*.
   C. Change *it's* to *its*.
   D. Make no change.

7. What changes, if any, are needed in line 20?
   A. Change *says* to *said*.
   B. Take out the word *would*.
   C. Change *says* to *said* and put the comma outside the quote marks.
   D. Make no change.

8. Which of the sentences in paragraph 5 could be left out?
   A. The last one.
   B. The third one.
   C. The second one.
   D. The first one.

GO ON

Passage B

Marco wrote the following book report for his social studies class. He has asked you to look it over before he hands it in.

Read the report carefully and help him improve his organization, revise his sentence structure, and correct his mechanics. Feel free to write in the text as you read, revise, and edit.

1   **The Titanic**

2   **A Book Report by Marco Pacheco**

3   The *Titanic* was the largest ship of its kind when it was launched in 1912.
4 Its owners claimed it was unsinkable. On the night of April 14th, it struck
5 an iceberg and sank in 2½ hours, proving that anything is sinkable. About
6 1,500 people lost their lives in the tragedy.

7   To this day, no one really knows what happened to the *Titanic*. For years,
8 people thought the iceberg had made a long gash on the ship's side. But, in
9 1986, another explanation was offered. Dr. Robert Ballard launched a robot
10 called Jason Jr. Jason Jr. went down to the bottom of the ocean where the
11 *Titanic* is. The robot entered the ship and took pictures of it. From the
12 pictures, it looks like the ship sank because the metal hull plates buckled
13 after hitting the iceberg. This let water into the ship. None of the photos
14 show a large rip that could have been made by an iceberg. There are
15 photos of objects lying on the ocean floor.

16   It starts with the history of the ship through its fateful maiden voyage.
17 It ends with the most recent findings as seen through the eyes of Jason Jr.
18 The best part of the book is the chapter on the passengers' stories. Society
19 at that time was so differant from what it is today. For instance, many
20 lifeboats were only half full because of the "women and children first"
21 rule. Even though there was room on the boats for more people, they
22 won't let the men on. I don't think this would happen today.

23   I enjoyed this book immensely. For some reason, I find myself fascinated
24 by this horrible tragedy. I also loved seeing the photos of how the ship
25 looked. It was very grand!

26   I would recommend this book to anyone interested in learning more
27 about the sinking of the unsinkable *Titanic*.

9. What editing change, if any, does Marco need to make in line 4 ("Its...unsinkable.")?
  A. Change *Its* to *It's*.
  B. Change *owners* to *owner's*.
  C. Change *it was* to *it's*.
  D. Make no change.

10. Which transition is needed at the beginning of the third sentence ("On...sinkable.")?
  A. Therefore,
  B. Because,
  C. Nevertheless,
  D. Moreover,

11. What is the BEST way to combine the ideas in the two sentences on lines 9-11 ("Dr. ...is.")?
  A. Dr. Robert Ballard launched a robot called Jason Jr. and Jason Jr. went down to the bottom of the ocean where the *Titanic* is.
  B. Dr. Robert Ballard launched a robot called Jason Jr., which went down to the bottom of the ocean where the *Titanic* is.
  C. A robot called Jason Jr. was launched by Dr. Robert Ballard to the bottom of the ocean where the *Titanic* is.
  D. Launched by Dr. Robert Ballard was Jason Jr., a robot that went down to the bottom of the ocean where the *Titanic* is.

12. You think Marco needs a transition sentence at the beginning of the third paragraph (line 16). Which sentence would be your choice?
  A. *The Titanic* is a very interesting book.
  B. The photos taken by Jason Jr. are very interesting.
  C. The legend is an incredible one.
  D. Every detail of the tragedy is included.

13. Which editing change, if any, should Marco make in the sentence in lines 18-19 ("Society...today.")?
  A. Change *Society* to *Sosiety*.
  B. Change *so* to *sew*.
  C. Change *differant* to *different*.
  D. Make no change.

14. What editing change, if any, is needed in lines 21-22 ("Even...on.")?
  A. Change *was* to *were*.
  B. Change *was* to *is*.
  C. Change *won't* to *can't*.
  D. Change *won't* to *wouldn't*.

15. Where should Marco move the sentences on lines 24-25 ("I...grand!")?
  A. after line 3 ("The...1912.")
  B. after lines 7-8 ("For...side.")
  C. after line 16 ("It...voyage.")
  D. Leave it where it is.

16. Which sentence would be the best to omit from the report?
  A. lines 5-6 ("About...tragedy.")
  B. lines 14-15 ("There...floor.")
  C. line 18 ("The...stories.")
  D. line 23 ("I...immensely.")

Passage C

Josh wrote this letter to Mr. McKinney, the principal of his school, to try to convince him to add another coach to the lacrosse team. He has asked you to check it before he sends it.

Read the letter carefully and help Josh improve his organization, revise his sentence structure, and correct his mechanics. Feel free to write in the text as you read, revise, and edit the letter.

1   April 13, 1999

2   Dear Mr. McKinney,

3   I am writing to ask you to reconsidar your decision to limit the number of
4   students on the lacrosse team.

5   This year 95 boys tried out for lacrosse; more than ever before. There is
6   only room for 40 students on the team. This means that, 55 boys who
7   want to play lacrosse can't. If you limit the number of team members to
8   30, as you've stated, an additional 10 students will not be able to play. You
9   are going against what you have told us.

10   Instead of limiting the team to 30 boys, why not add another coach?
11   Then you can increase the number of lacrosse players to 45. This gives
12   more boys an opportunity to play.

13   You have told us middle school is the time to explore things in order to
14   discover our likes and dislikes. By limiting the amount of lacrosse players,
15   you're preventing many students from trying out this sport.

16   Hiring a third coach will allow more students to discover lacrosse.
17   We know of one teacher who is willing to coach lacrosse. It would not be
18   a problem for you to find someone to take the job. The lacrosse team is
19   willing to hold fund-raisers.

20   We might like to meet with you to discuss this issue. Let us know when
21   would be the best time to do this.

22   Yours truly,

23   Josh Jacobs, Captain

24   Boy's Lacrosse Team

17. What editing change, if any, should Josh make in lines 3-4 ("I...team.")?
    A. Change *reconsidar* to *reconsider*.
    B. Change *decision* to *dicision*.
    C. Change *writing* to *writting*.
    D. Make no change.

18. What editing change, if any, should Josh make to line 5 ("This...before.")?
    A. Add a comma after *boys*.
    B. Change the semicolon to a comma.
    C. Change *more* to *More*.
    D. Make no change.

19. What would be a better location for the sentence in lines 8-9 ("You...us.")?
    A. after lines 3-4 ("I...team.")
    B. after line 10 ("Instead...coach?")
    C. after lines 14-15 ("By...sport.")
    D. after lines 17-18 ("It...job.")

20. What editing change, if any, should Josh make in lines 13-14 ("You...dislikes.")?
    A. Change *have* to *has*.
    B. Change *middle school* to *Middle School*.
    C. Change *things* to *thing*.
    D. Make no change.

21. Which transition is needed at the beginning of the sentence in lines 14-15 ("By...sport.")?
    A. Yet,
    B. First off,
    C. Therefore,
    D. Consequently,

22. Which is the BEST way to combine the two sentences in lines 17-18 ("We...job.")?
    A. We know of one teacher who is willing to coach lacrosse, so it would not be a problem for you to find someone to take the job.
    B. We know of one teacher who is willing to coach lacrosse, but it would not be a problem for you to find someone to take the job.
    C. It would not be a problem for you to find someone to take the job, knowing, as we do, of one teacher who is willing to coach lacrosse.
    D. We know of one teacher who is willing to coach lacrosse; however, it would not be a problem for you to find someone to take the job.

23. How would you revise the sentence in lines 18-19 ("The...fund-raisers.") to make the paragraph more logical?
    A. Although we won't be happy about it, the lacrosse team is willing to hold fund-raisers.
    B. In addition to getting another coach, the lacrosse team is willing to hold fund-raisers.
    C. The lacrosse team is eager to hold a fund-raiser.
    D. If money is a problem, the lacrosse team is willing to hold fund-raisers.

24. Which editing change, if any, should Josh make in the sentence on line 20 ("We...issue.")?
    A. Change *might* to *must*.
    B. Change *might* to *would*.
    C. Change *might* to *could*.
    D. Make no change.

GO ON

141

Passage D

Maria vacationed with her aunt and uncle this summer, so she wrote her aunt a thank you letter. She has asked you to look it over before she mails it.

Read the letter carefully and help her improve her organization, revise her sentence structure, and correct her mechanics. Feel free to write in the text as you read, revise, and edit.

1   July 25, 1999

2   Dear Aunt Dolores,

3   Thank you for the wonderful week I spent with you and Uncle Jim.

4   I really enjoyed the entire week. From the moment I arrived on Friday
5 evening, you make me feel special. The back yard barbecue was a great way
6 for me to meet people my own age in the neighborhood.

7   However, what I enjoyed most was the boat trip. Four days of sightseeing
8 by boat was like a dream come true. I loved the stops at each marina. Every
9 place that we visited was great. The restaurants, shops, and beaches were
10 all great. Shopping was the best. I love the swim wear we bought! That store
11 on the second marina was unique.

12   When I got home I couldn't wait to tell my parents what a wonderful
13 time I had. You gave me an exciting vacation.

14   Thank you again for inviting me. I am looking forward to next years
15 visit already.

16   Love from your neice,

17   Maria

25. What editing change, if any, should Maria make in line 3 ("Thank...Uncle Jim.")?
   A. Add a comma after *week*.
   B. Change *spent* to *spend*.
   C. Add *with* before *Uncle Jim*.
   D. Make no change.

26. What editing change, if any, is needed in lines 4-5 ("From...special.")?
   A. Change *arrived* to *arrive*.
   B. Change *make* to *made*.
   C. Change *feel* to *felt*.
   D. Make no change.

27. What editing change is needed in lines 5-6 ("The...neighborhood.")?
   A. Change *back yard* to *backyard*.
   B. Change *was* to *is*.
   C. Change *people* to *peeple*.
   D. Change *neighborhood* to *nieghborhood*.

28. What editing change, if any, is needed in lines 7-8 ("Four...true.")?
   A. Change *was* to *would be*.
   B. Change *was* to *were*.
   C. Change *was* to *is*.
   D. Make no change.

29. How can Maria BEST revise the sentences in lines 8-10 ("Every...great.")?
   A. The restaurants, shops, and beaches visited by us all were great.
   B. Every restaurant, shop, and beach that we visited was great.
   C. Every place that we visited was great; the restaurants, shops, and beaches were all great.
   D. I thought it was great that we visited restaurants, shops, and beaches.

30. What editing change is needed in lines 12-13 ("When...had.")?
   A. Change *got* to *get*.
   B. Change *couldn't* to *could'nt*.
   C. Change *parents* to *parents'*.
   D. Add a comma after *home*.

31. What editing change, if any, should Maria make in lines 14-15 ("I...already.")?
   A. Change *forward* to *forword*.
   B. Change *years* to *year's*.
   C. Change *already* to *all ready*.
   D. Make no change.

32. What editing change, if any, should Maria make in her closing (line 16)?
   A. love from your neice,
   B. Love from your niece,
   C. Love from your Niece,
   D. The closing is best as it is.

Writer's Checklist

Important Points to Remember as You Write and Critically Read to Revise/Edit Your Writing

Content/Organization

1. Focus on your purpose for writing and on your audience. Convince your audience that your point of view, solution, or causes and/or effects are reasonable.

2. Support your point of view, solution, or causes and/or effects with details and evidence.

3. Put your ideas in the order that best communicates what you are trying to say.

Sentence Construction

4. Use clear and varied sentences.

Usage

5. Use words correctly.

Mechanics

6. Capitalize, spell, and punctuate correctly.

7. Write neatly.